BACK PORCH MORNINGS

My Journey to Peace

By

Ageless Sage

Patricia Ely

ISBN: 1492180297

ISBN 13: 9781492180296

DEDICATION

This book is dedicated to my late husband, Milo, in memory of our love and all the potential that he helped me uncover within myself.

It is also dedicated to my sons, Michael and David, who left too soon. I will always hold both of you close to my heart.

ACKNOWLEDGEMENTS

I wish to acknowledge my good friends Kathy Duffy, Ellare Cortazzo, Turra Mauldin, and Rose Campbell. They have been steadfast across these years. We have laughed, we have cried and their support has brought me through it all. As well, their encouragement, suggestions and cheerleading helped greatly in the completion of this manuscript.

I want to acknowledge my grandchildren: Michael, Sheri, Beth, Haley, Seth, Noel, James, and Lauren; also, Allison, Lisa, Micaela, Melisa and Milo. You have all filled my "sageing" years with much joy. Love you all.

David, Susan, Bill and Barbara– thank you so much for your continuing love and support.

To Pam Thompson, my editor, my grateful thanks for all her able assistance, patience and understanding. Her suggestions and professional approach greatly improved my efforts.

TABLE OF CONTENTS

INTRODUCTION

*The real voyage of discovery
consists not in seeking new landscapes
but in having new eyes.*
Marcel Proust
In Search of Lost Time

As everyone does, I have come here to this experience to write the story of my life...a life that by now has been filled with love and joy, loss and pain and everything in between. I have chosen paths to walk that have brought me success and delight. There were other times that my choices didn't move me forward in a positive vein. Over the years, as I gained needed awareness I worked at switching tracks and moving more into where I believed I wanted to be. My life, just as yours, has never included the option of backing up to rewrite any script, redo any one event or relationship. In every instance I could only begin anew right where I was, regardless of where the years found me.

Time has passed far too quickly for me and life has produced profound changes that I could never have dreamed. There are benefits, as I find with aging I have gained wisdom and more time to do what brings me a greater sense of joy and satisfaction.

Of late I have discovered that sometimes all I am required to do is remove the dusty cover from long held interests. In addition, I have also dug deeper to uncover dreams and ideas too long buried under piles of responsibilities that took center stage for so many years.

I do not really see my life as being more unique or special than yours. It is just that I feel I seem to have finally been able to be more open to the opportunities that present themselves. I have also managed to weather the undeniable storms that have roared across these last few years.

So here I now sit, literally on the back porch of my life, waiting for that final sunset, knowing it approaches far too rapidly for my liking. In retrospect it has been an interesting trip. A majority of the last twenty plus years have found me searching for and finding a better fit for myself in this great experience called life. Once I began to really examine moving beyond the usual but constricting boundaries that I was raised with I discovered there were many other opportunities available. These would give me a deeper sense of purpose than I could have ever dreamed possible. Now I work every day to keep myself open to the positive that is always waiting for me.

Moving on into retirement years will find some with a death grip, hanging onto youth and the past. Much of our attitude can be influenced by the media and the image they too often project that tends to make us feel that aging is some awful mistake or great cosmic joke perpetrated by a God who thinks only youth has any value in today's world. Despite this view, others, myself included, sail along ready to embrace a new future. We may not be totally thrilled with the ever increasing number of wrinkles. Even I don't much care for that old woman who thinks she owns my mirror space these days. Many of us sixty and older, clocks ticking more loudly than ever, are living longer and healthier lives and seeking a place that reflects renewed or continued interest in all manner of activities. If we are willing to look with awareness, we can also find the long sought feeling of contentment and sense of peace that lies buried deep inside. Being one of the lucky ones, I have worked for many years to discover and hold onto these wonderful gifts that were there all along, just waiting for me to open the door.

Are you aware that you, too, with a little exploration and practice can discover this for yourself, if you have not already arrived? What is the story of your life and particularly now, how would you like to write the ending? Let's face it, these last years have all of us on a downhill skid! Do you feel this is depressing? Depends on how you choose to look at it.

Me, I'm working really hard to see how long I can outrun the end! Yes, I know it is coming and probably sooner than I would like. I also know that when that angel grabs me, he'll have to drag me out kicking and screaming, "Wait just a minute...I'm not done with" whatever I'm into at that moment. Most of those who know me would agree with that assessment.

So, where do you stand, fully present and actively engaged or just waiting to slip quietly out that final door? Or are you willing and interested in taking what time you have left to find and expand your joy?

It is neither practical nor necessary to reveal all the details of this long journey that have brought me to where I now find myself. I'm also sure that many have life experiences that would rival, if not surpass, mine. If there is a next time, maybe I'll be smarter, earlier, but what fun would that be?

In these pages I will share with you thoughts and feelings expressed in journal entries, as well as memories, bits of wisdom, and some heartfelt advice. May you find some gem that resonates with you and opens you to find the courage, the verve, to live out your remaining years with a little more inspiration, courage, joy, love and fun. Life, yours and mine, is not over until we draw our last breath. Let us continue to seek delight in the years we have left and be ever so grateful for all of it, large and small.

CHAPTER I

LEARNING TO SING MY SONG

If you ask me what I came
to do in this world,
I, an artist,
I will answer you:
I am here to live out loud.
Emile Zola
Writers on Writing

These days I maintain more strongly than ever that I do not want to die before my heart's song has been sung. In order to fulfill this promise to myself I have renewed my interest in any number of activities including Djembe hand drumming. Also a life-long love of singing prompted me to join the local community college choir. These are just two ways that I keep actively engaged. In addition I continue to pursue other interests that include writing, knitting, sewing and gardening. Group activities, friendships and family keep me socially connected. These all contribute to my physical, emotional and mental health.

More than twenty years ago I started a practice of journal writing, recording my thoughts, feelings, activities and poems. At the start I was not as aware of the benefits of a daily writing practice, as I am now. These books have accumulated into a much bigger stack than I could have once imagined. Reviewing them has revealed the insights and events that I recently realized have molded me into the "Ageless Sage" that I have now become.

The simple act of living beyond three quarters of a century has evolved me into a very different person than I was at 25 or even 40. I have been shaped by my innate nature as well as my habits and upbringing. Yet being no different than anyone else, I also am greatly impacted by my experiences, talents, and relationships. This includes being open to change and learning things that I was not taught as a child. I can be too quick to misjudge a new concept because it has not always been on my radar screen. Like many others, it is easy to reject anything new out of fear and narrowness of thinking.

As I have aged, a long held belief helped me to be more open to new ideas. I felt certain for so many years that there had to be more to life than what I was currently experiencing. A voice deep inside just kept prodding me to keep looking and that voice became louder as I grew older.

Initially I began my search as I left high school and home. When I still wasn't finding what I was looking for I thought that marriage might be the answer. Then I got busy raising a family and moving all over the country. As those events took precedence my search fell by the wayside.

In my early fifties, after so much living and trying and failing at relationships, I revitalized my search for deeper meaning. As the process began anew and I questioned life more deeply, I just knew that somehow there had to be something on a more profound level. I was convinced "it" was there somewhere reachable if I would just continue my search for the mystery.

A natural tendency, exhibited over much of the course of my adult life, is that I am brave enough to keep trying new things until I find a fit. For example, I began rollerblading in my mid-fifties and was thrilled to fly along on those inline skates for ten years. Now the only thing that keeps me off the wheels is artificial hips plus the look of absolute horror that registers on the surgeon's assistant's face whenever I dare mention such an activity.

Another thing that may have helped me to be more open was working on my college education for my BS and MA in my forties and fifties. I had to be willing to make more room in my thinking to understand the greater world and different cultures, sciences and ideas. Perhaps I am just naturally curious and more than willing to reach beyond the small-town mindset I grew up with.

I also see three other aspects as having major impacts on my life: being creative, a fast study and born under the astrological sign of Aries. I believe creative people are very open to alternate ways of looking at the world. If not, how would they ever create anything new or different? As a quick study, I can usually grasp elementary components easily enough to discern whether or not I want to dig deeper. Being a typical Aries, I am often impatient, sometimes too much so, to move on to the next new idea. I believe in the concepts of astrology and have discovered that the resulting influences of birth signs contain profound power.

It has amazed me to understand that the effects of being born at a given place, date and time shape various facets of my personality in so many ways. Much of who I am is related to this one factor. God made the world and everything in it very orderly and everyone benefits from the gifts of the natural cycles. Studying this ancient science has helped me to grasp concepts about myself and others at a much deeper level. I recommend that all of you, if you are not already familiar with your astrological sign, examine this subject. It will explain a great deal to you about your personality traits.

In the past I had been a Catholic and then a Lutheran after being raised Episcopalian. Initially immersing myself in each, I would forget about my original search for a time. Eventually I did find what I was seeking but it turned out to be beyond the confines of any formal religion.

After yet another failed relationship I began to examine in deeper detail other aspects of spirituality that lay beyond the walls of organized religion. Quickly I realized that what I sought for so long was within reach. Enjoying my new found knowledge I read widely to grasp a better understanding of all these individuals who, over years and centuries, were able to tap into the real wisdom of the Universe.

More years would pass before I came to realize that I found more peace in my "back porch mornings" than I was able to find in any church pew I ever occupied. My conclusion became, and I am not unique in this assessment, no one has all the answers and don't let anyone persuade you otherwise.

Please understand that I have nothing against any religious affiliation. Everyone is entitled to be part of what provides them with their own best relationship with our Creator. We all deserve to find our own path, our own place of peace.

Sadly, many don't even realize such a place is available. It is possible to get stuck along the road of life that may be filled with rocks and ruts. Too often there also can be an occasional large hole where we easily get lost. But no challenge is too great if you have faith in a Higher Power and yourself.

Personally I am convinced that God really doesn't mind what you call Him/Her be it God, Loving Universe, Messiah, or any of the titles used over the centuries. Regardless of what I came to believe in my childhood, I no longer think that God or his angels sit up there on a cloud somewhere, writing down every one of our misdeeds. There is no storage place that saves these for the day we come face to face.

The important thing is to acknowledge that there is an all-powerful, loving, healing Presence that accepts us all, every last one of us, just as we are. He is always available to help and guide us, no matter where we are in any given moment of our lives. The really important step is to reach out, to ask for the help that we need.

As we all walk through life in our own way, sometimes we have blinders on and sometimes we are more open to what the world has to offer. But we never get to do it all and there are many, I think, who never manage to move beyond just the basics of everyday living.

With aging, it seems to me to be more important than ever to decide to pursue what really matters to each of us. Some have health limitations. Too many, particularly older women, have financial constraints that limit options. Still, there are ways to find enjoyable pursuits even on a restricted budget, if we take time and effort to look.

Maybe we didn't plan better for this because we didn't believe that we would ever be left here to take care of ourselves. Certainly, my generation of girls who would become wives and mothers were basically brought up to believe that our husbands would always be here and provide for us. In days long past there were not nearly the career options open to women that exist today. The results were not only lost wages but unused talents and unexpanded horizons.

The current challenges have, at this point, most likely moved away from earning a living and raising children, to surviving the remaining years. If at all possible, the focus should now turn to how to best relish what is left, find our song and wrap ourselves in the peace that we have earned. The answer will be different for all of us, as will the roads that lead us each in our own direction.

I can only share with you my successes and failures. Don't be afraid to try and fail, even as you age. Regardless of your years, I cannot encourage you too much to begin the journey to discover what resonates in the deepest part of your soul. No matter how young or old you are, you can do it and you really are worth it! You will find that it is way more interesting than parking yourself in front of mindless TV day after day or sitting around consumed by constant complaining. If I can continue on this path, why can't you?

No one, especially the young or even the middle aged, understands what it is like to be in this place. We are all forever 35 somewhere deep inside, often unable and/or unwilling to acknowledge that we can no longer do _____ (you fill in the blank). I don't like it either. I wanted to be forever in my fifties and sixties. I had just hoped to be a little wiser and happier as I was coming truly into my own place after all the years of dealing with uncertainty and struggle.

Therefore, I have now promised myself that I will write, drum and sing for as long as I can, and I am willing to add to that list anything else that most appeals to me. I still look for opportunities to experience more of what life offers. I would like to learn to tap dance, kayak, and go hang-gliding. I'll probably think of a few more before I leave. Some of my friends think I'm crazy but that is okay; nearly all my life I've been seen as a little strange.

What is your promise to yourself? Hopefully, within these pages that draw a picture of me, something, some few words, an idea, perhaps a silly line, will crack open the door to your more joyous self. So much remains in life to be explored. I truly hope that you can be kind to yourself and find new ways to experience more while you are still here. Never mind what anyone else thinks. If you can't find someone to share the adventure, start out alone. You will find plenty of like-minded souls along the road who will be happy you joined them.

CHAPTER II

MY JOURNEY

There is a vitality, a life force, an energy, a quickening that is translated through you into action. And because there is only one of you in all of time, this expression is unique, and if you block it, it will never exist through any other medium and it will be lost.
Martha Graham
Quotations Book

My background has included a most ordinary life in some ways for I was raised in a small town surrounded by a family that included my parents and two siblings. I was the girl filling in the sandwich framed by my brothers. I also was fortunate to have both sets of my grandparents as well as all my mother's brothers and sisters and my dad's brother. They were all involved in my growing years.

My earliest memories started when I was two. I am certain of that because I remember being at my maternal grandmother's house when my father called to tell her my baby brother was born. He was 25 months younger than me.

Until I was 17 we lived behind my father's parents' home in a small house that I was told over the years, was a converted chicken coop. It is plausible because my grandfather did have a barn with a cow and for a while, a donkey, or small horse that pulled a cart we rode in as young children. There also were lots of chickens in a much larger barn. These were chickens my parents raised, butchered and sold. (Anyone else remember the smell of singed chicken feathers?)

By the time I was a senior in high school we moved into a sprawling ranch house my father built on the other side of town. It was across the crick as we were known to say. He always insisted on painting it flamingo pink!

From early on I loved to write. It seems to come far more easily to me now. For as long as I can remember I have written poetry. In high school I wrote articles for the newsletter. Over the years I have written and edited many newsletters for various groups.

Following high school graduation, I went to Drexel Institute in Philadelphia. My goal was to become a fashion journalist. I loved clothes and still do. When I was quite young my mother once said to me, "You'd wear your best dress out to hang up the wash, if I would let you." Truly she was right; I still prefer to dress up.

Difficult circumstances reared their ugly heads and I ended up in the Boston area for a number of years. This was the beginning of my doing a lot of things I didn't really like to do, such as waitressing and clerical work, just to keep food on the table. Years later following divorce, it would become a repeated but necessary pattern as I often raised my sons alone.

I met my first husband when I worked at a restaurant just outside of Harvard Square. After marriage and another year or so of living near Boston, we relocated to El Paso, Texas for his work as a civilian contractor at Fort Bliss. It was the beginning of a pattern of moving every year. My husband was assigned to Strategic Air Command bases to train the military and the contracts for his job were revised annually.

Our older son, Michael was born in El Paso in 1960. Another move found us near Detroit and 23 months apart to the very day in 1962, our other son David was born. Other moves found us in Arizona, Iowa, California and Ohio.

The most difficult aspect of such frequent moves was the hardship of only being in each location for such a short time. This made it nearly impossible to form any kind of friendships. I was a very long way from family and almost never had a car. My husband traveled, sometimes for extended periods. With one and then two toddlers, I often felt very isolated. Living coast to coast and border to border was not necessarily as great an adventure as it could have been under different circumstances.

While living in Ohio, my husband decided to reenlist in the army and was shipped overseas. I moved back to my hometown until the boys and I could receive travel papers. The military had not issued concurrent ones for us that would have enabled us to travel with him to Germany. Unfortunately, being the severe alcoholic and gambler that he was, he never sent us any money. I was forced to go to work so I could feed Michael and David. Within a year I had found a job, filed for divorce and worked to move on with my life.

The three of us lived in an apartment for two or three years but the owners said they were going to sell the building and suggested I relocate. Behind the grade school that was attended by three generations of my family, I found a 100-year-old house that hadn't been occupied for a couple of years. The owner agreed to rent it to us, and I painted most of the rooms before we moved in. Being such an old house without central heat and no basement, it had one small gas heater in the living room. There was no heat at all on the second floor.

Three or four years later, on a freezing wintery February day, my father was there, trying to thaw my frozen water pipes and the house caught fire. While the fire was raging, a neighbor was able to locate me at work about a ½ hour away. (My mother said she was waiting to see how much damage there was before calling me!) I rushed home and will never forget how I felt when I saw the dining room curtains that I had worked so hard to buy, blowing out the smoky, broken windows. When I walked up the hill to the house I found my dad, in his firemen's vest, the front covered in ice. The fire seemed to smolder forever.

The firemen had a really difficult time putting the blaze out. They had to run their hoses from a hydrant some distance away, up the hill. Old newspapers stored in the crawlspace attic were impossible to reach and continued to burn for hours. Eventually the roof caved in across the back of the house over the bathroom and my boys' bedroom. I was so eternally grateful that we were not home sleeping when the fire started. Under the actual circumstances, I don't believe it was a real concern. We lost nearly everything but our dog, Crossy.

Left with only the clothes we wore that day and little else, we were in shock. We were not able to assess the damage until the next day. So little was left to be recovered and going inside was dangerous. The stairs to the second floor were badly burned and very risky to climb. Still, with great bravery David managed to get into their bedroom safely enough to recover Michael's first toy, a rubberized Snoopy dog. Years later when Michael died, his kids gave it to David as a keepsake. What was left of the house was later torn down.

For the first time in my life I deeply came to understand that the world stops for nothing, no matter how great the tragedy or who you are. However, I was determined that this loss would not defeat me and I repeated that sanity saver like a mantra for a very long time.

I was profoundly moved by the kindnesses that many showered us with, friends, family and strangers alike. Donations of clothing, money and furniture poured in. All these enabled us to set up a new living space and move back into daily routines.

Michael seemed to be most affected by the events, waking me nightly to say his bedroom was too hot and he was afraid it would catch fire. He was definitely traumatized by being forced to watch the house burn from his fourth grade classroom window. His teacher just didn't seem to have enough common sense to remove him from this terrible vantage point.

My deepest concern was to somehow put our lives back in order and be able to move past this tragedy. How I held it all together and kept going is a good question. Am I simply made of some stronger inner strength? Or was it just the desire to shuffle all the pieces back into place for the sake of Michael and David? It could have been both and more. One thing is for certain, my heritage holds a lot of strong people who always kept going even under even the most difficult circumstances. I am certain it all combined to move me along. I simply refused to surrender to the loss.

Time moved on and so did we, through another marriage and divorce, new living spaces and jobs, and three years of full-time college for me. In 1978 I summoned up enough courage to move to Pittsburgh. Michael wanted to attend an automotive mechanic school there and David was getting into too much trouble with alcohol and drugs. By this time I was in my last year at the University of Pittsburgh, Bradford, and my job had been dissolved, again. It always seemed that, as needed, if I wouldn't move myself along, the Universe stepped in to force the issue. The relocation would benefit all of us.

Before we made the shift I found a new job and a new place to live. We settled in and adjusted as Michael enrolled and completed his training. Still in high school, David had to repeat his sophomore year. He received a great deal of needed encouragement from a faculty member who was the football coach and a teacher at his new school. He was also motivated enough to apply for college while in his senior year. The spring after our move I graduated from the University of Pittsburgh, summa cum laude, with a Bachelor's degree in Psychology. David did start there in engineering following high school graduation, but he dropped out at the end of his first year, a decision he always regretted.

The years passed with more moves, jobs, and relationships for all of us. By 1982, I was getting married again and the grandchildren began arriving until I had eight. I never realized how much joy all of them would bring into my life. Maybe it was because I could take more time to appreciate them than when I was raising my own children. Now I was no longer struggling to feed a family. I had only myself to worry about and for several years I actually had a decent job. I know it has been said before, but grandchildren give us many opportunities to see the world through their young eyes, all over again. All of them are unique, and I still enjoy them today. Of course, with some of them married I am now blessed

with nine great-grandchildren. I also have gained four stepchil-
dren and their sons and daughters.

We all have a history when we reach this age. As you can see, mine
has not been all that unusual so I will spare you any more details.

It just wasn't possible for me to realize how much more my world
was going to open up and that it would be so different, so much
better than the first 56 years. Life offers you surprises when
you least expect them. A great deal of happiness was waiting
in the wings, as well as continued spiritual growth and insight.
Obviously for me at least, the real gems were soon to be uncovered.
The coming years would not solve all my problems, but would lead
to greater self-acceptance as well as deeper understanding and
spirituality. I was totally unaware that I was also on the brink of
receiving two of the greatest gifts of my life. A future was waiting
patiently for me that would prove to be far more meaningful than
I could ever dream

CHAPTER III

MY GREATEST GIFTS

You are willing to read my soul
And not just poke at my mind
As so many others have done,
Afraid, even there, of what they might find.
When you can truly know who I am
Will you still want to share my space
As you learn what lies within
And sustains me in this deep, holy place?
Will your courage last to carry you past
All the distractions, the din and the strife
Your heart daring to find the real me
That is meant to bloom in this life?
Ageless Sage

At this point I had been alone for four-and-a-half years following another, most painful divorce, never dating anyone. My time was well filled with my job and grandchildren. I also went back to school. At the end of two years I had earned a Master's Degree in Journalism and Communications, graduating in 1991. When I decided to continue my education I found Point Park College had an excellent program that worked really well for mature students with jobs. I even completed my thesis before graduation, only because I knew if I lost my momentum I would never finish it.

Now it was my birthday and I had no one to celebrate with. In searching for a way to mark the occasion on my own, I heard about a lecture at what was then the Sheraton Inn. It was being presented by Scott Peck, author of *The Road Less Traveled*. This was a book I had found insightful so off I went, departing straight from work, the distance far enough that I would only be able to get there in time for the presentation. Supper would have to wait.

I arrived on time, registered, and went to find a seat. I sat down next to an attractive older gentleman. Tall, white-haired and with very blue eyes, dressed in a suit and a red tie, he looked interesting. Alas, I felt too awkward to say anything. In a room full of strangers I always have to struggle to fit in and be comfortable with light chit-chat; one-on-one with those I know, I am much more sociable.

Near the beginning of the lecture, we were instructed to introduce ourselves to the person on our right and tell them a little about ourselves, if possible, something unusual. Since I have always felt it was my greatest, most difficult achievement, I told him I had learned how to fly a single-engine plane. Whatever he may have revealed to me is long forgotten except he said he had been in the Navy during WWII and had a degree in engineering.

I sensed I would like to know more for he certainly provoked my curiosity. After the lecture he invited me for coffee at a local restaurant. I told him that I needed to have something more substantial as I had skipped dinner in order to arrive on time. I ended up eating breakfast, which we always joked about later as it was my birthday "dinner."

We talked for a long time, trading information. At some point Milo wanted to know how old I was. I told him that it was actually my birthday and I was 57. Not until we were ready to say goodnight was I able to persuade him to admit that he was 72. I think he thought I would find him too old. Frankly, from that very first day, the age factor never bothered me. Until near the very end of his life he always seemed so ageless. He was widowed; I was divorced.

Before we went our separate ways we exchanged phone numbers. We also agreed to go out the end of the following week for dinner and a movie. From that day on, I would find myself in one of the most amazing relationships of my life. I did not realize it, but an experience like no other was starting. This relationship, the absolutely best one of my life, would continue for not nearly enough years, ending just 6 weeks short of 18 years when Milo passed. Now, it continues with him in spirit.

We were just two ordinary people, both unsure for far too long about a solid commitment, struggling with our individual fears and baggage from previous relationships. I had two sons from my first marriage and he had two sons and a daughter from his many years of marriage. It would be some time before all the introductions were accomplished. That was okay because neither of us was in a hurry to think of ourselves as a committed couple.

As our relationship evolved, we increasingly saw more of each other. We spent many hours hiking trails at Linn Run, Laurel Highlands, Ohiopyle and other interesting places. Often his daughter Susan had good suggestions, as she was and still is a very experienced trail hiker. We also attended weekend festivals and fairs where they had displays of old farm machinery as well as maple syrup making demonstrations in the spring. On those rare occasions when the opportunity arose, we went to listen to bagpipe bands.

Milo began his love affair with the pipers years before when the bagpipe band would practice outside his dorm window. He studied engineering at Carnegie Mellon when it was a tech school.

Three times I hired bagpipers to play for him. For his eightieth birthday a piper came to the house and played, standing on the front walk. Most of the neighbors came out to listen. He told me he never had a better birthday gift. Ten years later his birthday was the same day as his family reunion. I was able to find a piper in the Franklin area willing to come out to the 4H meeting hall to play for him. After he was honored, he had the shortsightedness to ask me who hired the piper! As if he couldn't figure it out! At his graveside on a freezing February day, I had another piper play one last moving tribute.

In the early stages of our hiking days I frequently worried and fretted about my two sons and their families. Always feeling responsible for everyone and everything since childhood, I felt that I should be able to fix all the problems that they faced. When we were together, Milo came up with a unique solution. I lived in one county, he in the next. When he would come to fetch me he would tell me, as we crossed the county line driving east, "Now you are in Westmoreland County. Leave your problems in Allegheny County where they belong." I learned to do just that.

That initial meeting in 1993 turned into our many years of being together. We enjoyed just sharing time, hiking and other outdoor activities. Often we would walk at Twin Lakes, a place where there are walking paths around both lakes. We also canoed there and at Lake Arthur a few times.

The canoe outings were always enjoyable regardless of the fact that I seemed to do most of the paddling. Being the old Navy man that he was, Milo maintained that he helped with the most important part...the steering. He probably was right, as I had no idea how to stay the course. To my delight, on such exquisitely peaceful outings, I always felt like an old Indian gliding silently across the water.

Milo had a great liking for old trains and steam engines, in particular. One fall we made a trip to West Virginia and took advantage of a day ride on a train made up of old passenger cars and powered by a steam engine. We had a most interesting trip viewing the fall foliage through the New River Gorge. Our seats were in a car with domed windows which afforded a magnificent view.

When the weather turned cold we really enjoyed Milo's fireplace. We also shared mutually agreeable pursuits like crossword puzzles. Much of our time was spent doing simple things, enjoying the quiet and each other. We actually reached a point where we were so tuned in to one another that one of us would finish the other's sentences or he would bring up the exact thing that I was considering in my mind. I could often turn the tables and do it for him as well.

In April, 1998, Milo had a heart attack. We had been hiking earlier that day in Laurel Mountains. We had even veered off the beaten path. He later told me that he had not been feeling all that well most of the weekend. This was the reason he had returned home a day early from a trip to visit his brothers. Why he had decided to drive out to the mountains on this pleasant spring afternoon when he had such misgivings about how he was feeling, I never did understand.

After our return home and as our evening progressed, it became obvious that Milo was in even greater distress. I finally convinced him to let me call an ambulance. Off to the emergency room we went. They confirmed that he had suffered another heart attack. He had recovered from a previous one experienced some years before I met him. I got him settled in the cardiac care unit. Because it was now after midnight he made me agree not to call his family until morning. I went in to check on him early the next day. After a short time, he shooed me out, saying he just wanted to rest.

At this point, I needed to call his family. When I reached his daughter, Susan, at work, she told me she had just gotten a call from the hospital, telling her that her dad had had another episode and they were taking him into surgery, to do a heart catheterization and implant a stent. I rushed back to the hospital to join Milo's son Bill, Bill's fiancée, Chris Ann and Susan, to await the outcome. When the doctor came out he told us that Milo had 100% blockage in one artery and so they had imserted a stent.

Within a few days Milo was ready to be discharged and eager to return home. I told his family that I would stay with him until he recovered enough to be alone. I worked near the house and had more flexible hours than Susan and Bill. His son David lived out of state. This arrangement worked out well, as he was on a lot of medication and his recovery was very slow. Thus, it was even more important to have someone there every day to make sure that he ate regularly and well.

During his recovery from his heart problems, Milo finally allowed me to cook for him, which was a relief. His version of homemade soup was a can of Dinty Moore beef stew with a little water and a big bag of frozen, mixed soup vegetables. On a cold winter's night it could be alright, but mine, made from "scratch" as my grandmothers would say, was tastier and he admitted that I was the better cook.

In the beginning Milo had a difficult time, allowing me to do anything for him, even making him a cup of tea. He only accepted this if I was *already* going to the kitchen. I think he was afraid of becoming dependent on me. At that time neither of us had the slightest clue what the future would place on our plates or how lasting our relationship might be. I continued to do things for him, and in the end, I think I had him spoiled. He seemed content with the results.

My stay turned into weeks, then months and finally a year. At that point I realized I had not stayed at my apartment one single night for six months.

I told him, "Either I will move in here or go home and stay there. I am spending a lot of money on a place I am not living in."

His reply was, "I'm not sure I want a long-term relationship."

My response was, "If five years isn't long-term, I don't know what is."

After living with Milo for a time, I came to a new realization. While sitting on the back porch one summery Sunday morning writing in my journal, I had a revelation. It occurred to me that for the first time in my entire life I was with someone who not only allowed me to be me, but accepted and approved of the person that I was. He never once told me it was not a good idea to think or act in a certain way or that anything I did was wrong. He simply was in favor of the person that I was, no ifs, buts, or any demands on his part that I should be different. He certainly encouraged me to pursue any interest that I had. I could scarcely believe my good fortune!

All of my life I had viewed myself as being unacceptable and unloved. I felt like the black sheep who just never fit in anywhere. I think about the time I moved to Pittsburgh, I realized that I just had to go on, accept and learn to love the woman I had become. As I grew to understand that I truly was not such a bad person, I stopped worrying about what others thought. Still, when I believed that the unacceptance and disapproval included my own family, it made for a very lonely existence. No marriage had provided what I needed either. Someone was always trying to change who I was, always working at making me over. Awakening to this new perspective, it became my greatest gift. Eventually, I would come to realize more and more, that Milo himself was an even greater gift. His intelligent, loving, quiet presence in my life over these years that were now adding up, provided me with this wonderful present.

Milo had such a high level of curiosity. If I became interested in something that was new to him, he would always say, "Tell me more." I would read to him from some of the books that I was perusing to explore new subjects, or I would talk with him about the classes I was taking.

He was open to talking about anything with anyone, never putting a single person down or making them feel inferior. Milo's high level of curiosity made him more than willing to hear someone's "story." He had more patience than I would ever be able to scrape together in a lifetime of trying but my level did greatly increase with his influence.

From the very beginning of our relationship, Milo strongly maintained that he had absolutely no desire to marry again. I was not inclined to try again, either. I felt I had followed that path one too many times already. Still, he continued to ask me now and then if I was interested. I always said no, and he would affirm that he hadn't changed his mind. Evidently, failing to be the quick study that I can be, I was too dense to realize that he was actually testing my waters as he was becoming more inclined, for some reason, to consider such an option. We sure played that song over and over for a few years.

When I looked back in my journals, I found as time went on, I did begin to question whether or not I might want to marry Milo. I seemed to be moving toward a "yes," as well.

For so much of my life, virtually anything that I had ever asked for had been denied me. At a fairly young age I learned to depend on myself or do without. It truly was unusual for me to be able to voice my wants and needs. Then one spring day it seemed overwhelmingly important for me to ask for what I most desired. As my birthday approached Milo wanted to know what I would like to have for a gift. I told him that what I most desired was a ring so I would always have a significant reminder of him.

His response was, "A wedding ring?"

Because I was really nervous and intent on being so brave, I missed the cue.

Off I went to search for what I wanted and quickly found an exquisite little ring in the local Irish shop. Milo then went with me to purchase it and promptly put it on my left hand. Still, I wasn't getting the message!!!

About two months later, a friend urged me to get in touch with my true desires, and find my long stifled voice. It would be essential to do those things before I could ask for what it was I honestly wanted. When I followed this advice, I made a new decision.

A couple of days later on a Sunday afternoon, when we were sitting on the front porch swing, I said, "Well, do you want to go to Somerset and get a license or just go to West Virginia and get it over with?"

We quickly agreed on West Virginia. I arranged all the details. The following Wednesday we made the trek to Wheeling and got married by a judge in the courthouse. I know I wondered why we had not done it sooner and I believe he felt the same way.

By late fall Milo's health and eyesight were both failing but he never complained. Having lived in the same house for so many years he knew his way around. Needed hand rails, etc., were added so he could manage more easily. He adapted to his limits and I became a caregiver.

As always, we existed in love and patience, blending these new changes into the fabric of our lives. We seldom exchanged a cross word acknowledging that although there were things we would never agree on, we would not allow them to come between us.

He became frailer and I picked up the slack. It helped that he could still take care of his personal needs most of the time. There was a short period when I needed to help him get dressed and undressed in the mornings and evenings but eventually he regained enough strength to once again manage most things himself.

I read the newspaper to him as he ate his breakfast. Together we worked the crossword puzzles at dinner. I also read to him from books that we both found to be of interest.

Then two events occurred that really stressed our lives. I finally received ownership of my father's house in 2008. Because it was a three-and-a-half hour drive it was essential that I be able to go there for at least two or three days at a time in order to make any kind of progress. Until I gained access to the house I had no idea what a mess had been left for me. Months would pass before it was cleared out.

Being away for days at a time would mean that I had to find someone to come in and fix Milo's meals. I was not too concerned about leaving him alone during the day. He slept a lot, and usually was only up and around for breakfast and supper and some of the evening hours. His daughter Susan agreed to fill in, if I could make the trips on weekends. I also hired someone who lived nearby to help out on the rare occasion when Susan could not cover for me.

By the time I started to empty Dad's house, my hips were beginning to give me serious problems. Journal entries confirm that the onset of pain and difficulty walking was much earlier than I remembered. I have such a tendency to ignore my own health problems and just try, as best as I can, to plow ahead. I tend to have faith that somehow it will either be resolved by something I am doing or just go away.

As always, I tried all the natural remedies and healings available, hoping to experience relief. My walking became more difficult every day. Too soon I became bent over due to the extreme pain. At the most difficult point I really believed that I would never be able to stand up straight again.

In the spring of 2009, I talked to a doctor. Told I needed hip replacements I went into total denial. I do not do surgery well due to the anesthetics, nor am I highly in favor of invasive procedures. I don't even take prescription medicine without a battle and most of the time I still win that one. Finally I said, "What are you doing to yourself?" At that point I realized I was not going to be able to keep doing what I needed to do. The pain was becoming just so great that every single step was agony. Looming in my future was the prospect of ending up in a wheelchair. If that happened I knew I would never be able continue to manage my husband's care.

All the time away, and all the ramifications of the extreme pain took a toll on us. I had so wanted to take Milo to the beach that spring of 2009 after being apart so much over the course of the previous year. My thought was that just spending two weeks together without all the distractions would help us get re-established, somehow back to where we had been. However, I quickly came to see that it was no longer a plausible plan. My pain had become so great I could barely walk, and it became very difficult for me to even lift and carry a basket of laundry. I was disheartened that this special time together could not become a reality.

Now it was early summer and I could not even work in my gardens. I barely managed to meet my husband's needs on a daily basis. It took every ounce of grit I could muster just to get his food from the stove to the table. Milo didn't realize the amount of difficulty I was having, and I did not want him to know for there was no advantage in making him worry.

Due to end stage Glucoma, he had not been able to see out of his right eye at all for the past few years. The vision in his left eye was extremely limited. Since his sight was so affected, he could see almost nothing. Therefore Milo had no idea of my mobility struggles. He just knew I had a lot of pain.

Reluctantly, I talked to a surgeon and was told that I had necrosis, (the bone was dying) and that was what caused the pain. Still, I delayed the operations.

Years before, a major surgery had required six long months of recovery time. For someone so accustomed to constant activity and moving fast, you have no idea what an ordeal such a slow return to good health could mean. I honestly thought I would never get better at that time. I certainly was not interested in a repeat.

Milo's ninetieth birthday would be on the same day as his family reunion. I intended to hire another bagpiper to play for this milestone occasion. Certainly I did not want him to miss the reunion. Therefore I delayed my surgery because I had no way of knowing how fast, or slow, my recovery would be and whether or not I would be able to drive us there.

The original reunion had been initiated by Milo. He grew up with several brothers. As each sibling turned fifty, there was a big family party. Milo was the youngest and when it became his turn for the big half century celebration, he suggested that they all come together every year to acknowledge something other than funerals and weddings, and so the reunion was born. His birthday usually occurred near Labor Day. It was an easy decision to plan the annual reunion for the Saturday of the first weekend in September.

I was so glad that he was able to go that year. It did turn out to be the last reunion he would feel strong enough to attend.

In preparation for my surgeries, I knew I would need to hire someone to help with the caregiving and my recuperation. Ellare entered our lives then and we became good friends. Imagine my astonishment when I found out she was the widow of the teacher/coach who had so greatly influenced my son David years earlier when we moved to the area.

Ellare turned out to be an absolutely wonderful caregiver, and I quickly realized we were both in good hands when she was here. She was just so patient and kind and could pace her steps to Milo's needs, as well as being a most able help through both of my hip surgeries. Susan filled in on weekends, and as needed, and was also a great help, always so good to both of us. The two of them continued their caregiving for as long as we needed them.

Recovering so quickly from the first hip replacement, I was more than anxious to undergo the second one. The repaired hip made my leg two or three inches longer than the other, and I went around for those ensuing months wearing two different shoes so that I wouldn't walk with such a pronounced limp.

Exactly four months later, the other hip replacement was accomplished. I am so lucky because those two surgeries gave my life back to me. I can do nearly anything I want again, including running up and down ladders to paint rooms with nine-foot ceilings. Well, maybe not running but I can climb with the best of them.

I would still have my husband for just a bit more than a year after my second surgery in 2010. Because I just wanted our life together to get back on track, I was perhaps unable to acknowledge that our time together was becoming so short. But how can anyone know what the days and months ahead hold? We just went on, working the ins and outs of daily living.

However by late spring and into the summer, I could see a difference in Milo's mobility. He was becoming lost in the house and having more difficulty just getting around. I found I was not as comfortable leaving him during the day, even if he was resting in bed. I shortened my trips as much as possible when doing errands and begged him to stay put if I wasn't home when he woke.

Spring slid into summer and only twice or so was I able to coax Milo to sit on the front porch to enjoy the sun. Because going anywhere began to take so much of his short supply of energy, leaving the house had turned into an ordeal. I don't think he missed having to put forth the effort. He no longer wanted to ride in the car for any reason. He had developed a serious problem with nausea. I couldn't even take him to the barber for a haircut because he became so ill.

Thankfully, I was able to move around more with my new hips. I kept busy with gardens long neglected from two summers that had taken my energy elsewhere. As Milo was became increaseingly reclusive and withdrawn, I felt more and more alone. I wondered later if he had become depressed by his growing inability to do very much of anything and the continued decline of his eyesight. I honestly believe by that time he had lost what little remaining sight he had in his left eye, making him totally blind.

The days crawled by as summer melted into September and for the first time ever, Milo missed the family reunion. It just was no longer workable for us to make the trip.

Truly the years with this wonderful man that I had come to love so much blessed me with not one but two tremendously wonderful gifts. Our love made such a difference in our lives together and I was able to grow into the person that I was meant to become from the very beginning. I know I can never replace him, and often told him that he had spoiled me. I would never expect to be able to find another partner like him.

We don't ever get to have anyone in our lives forever because it is for certain that one of us, one day, just won't be physically present anymore. I treasure the time we had and will never forget it, but life also moves us in odd directions sometimes. Who knows where I will find myself in the future? Milo, himself, was truly the greatest birthday present I ever received. His total acceptance of me was an equally great gift.

It is my sincere hope that I have explained this well enough that you can understand what was so important to me. Many people share great love affairs with their partners, so it can be easier to understand that aspect of my gift. Perhaps only those who have gained that so important sense of their own value after years of searching can fully appreciate the other half of this equation. I truly wish both blessings for all of you.

CHAPTER IV

MY LOSSES BEGIN

The World breaks everyone,
And afterwards, some are
strong at the broken places.
Ernest Hemingway
A Farewell To Arms

DAD

In 2004, my father passed away. Ailing for a number of years with the increasingly debilitating effects of Alzheimer's and rapidly heading toward kidney failure as a result of large doses of diuretics, it was a blessing. At nearly 88, well loved by family and friends, he had lived a long life filled with great experiences. In his later years, he told me that he thought he had lived a most unexpectedly amazing life.

I hated to lose him as he and I were all that was left of the original family of five. Because of my mother's jealousy, we never really had the opportunity to appreciate and enjoy each other until after she passed away nearly twenty years earlier. We did make up for lost time as much as we could.

Dad was gregarious and loved talking with others and swapping stories. He never hesitated to give advice on his treasured methods of doing anything relating to fishing and hunting. However, he was extremely reluctant to reveal the best spots for either activity. An avid hunter and fisherman, he was well known for his hilarious tales, various adventures, sense of humor and great laugh. I always said his laugh started at his toes and worked its way out into a huge roar.

Over the years my dad had managed two different businesses from an office in his home. The first one, H.G. German's Seeds, was a wholesale/retail flower and vegetable seed company, started in 1926 by his father, Harry German. It was successfully operated for nearly sixty years before it was sold outside of the family. The company slogan had been "German's Seeds Germinate."

Dad had no college education but put forth tremendous effort to learn everything he could from those already established as growers and seedsmen. As a result, my father built his life's work into a million-dollar success. In 1987 he was recognized by Michigan State University with their Distinguished Service Award "as a world renowned horticulturist and seedsman" at their annual meeting of International Seedsmen. Held in East Lansing, those in attendance included many growers and seed company executives from American companies, as well as 75 people from Holland, England, Germany, Japan and South America.

After the seed business was gone and my mother had passed away, Dad turned to his hobby of tying fishing flies. He quickly expanded his talents into a full-fledged business, complete with his hand-tied flies and related supplies, including lots of feathers which always fascinated me. Over time, as his Alzheimer's progressed, business declined when too many buyers began to take advantage of his confusion, picking up far more goods than they had purchased.

Near the end, even when he couldn't say my name anymore, it was obvious from the big smile on Dad's face that he still knew who I was. The last time I saw him, he was in the hospital, almost totally incoherent and mentally confused during much of the visit. Dad was not permitted to have anything to eat or drink. As he was very thirsty, I gave him a water soaked sponge to suck. He had a grand time, teasing me by refusing to let go, gripping it in his teeth and shaking his head, almost laughing.

When I got ready to leave, I kissed him goodbye. Dad opened his eyes, looked at me and said, very plainly, "Just forget we were ever here." A couple of weeks later he was gone. I knew I would miss him terribly. For a long time, the opportunity to visit with him was usually the only reason I was willing to make the trip back home.

Years before he died Dad asked me to read *Do Not Stand At My Grave And Weep* by Mary Elizabeth Fry at his funeral and naturally I was willing to do so.

> Do not stand at my grave and weep
> I am not there. I do not sleep.
> I am a thousand winds that blow,
> I am the diamond glint on snow.
> I am the sunlight on ripened grain.
> I am the gentle autumn rain.
> When you awaken in the morning's hush. I am
> the swift uplifting rush
> Of quiet birds in circled flight.
> I am the soft stars that shine at night.
> Do not stand at my grave and cry;
> I am not there. I did not die.
> I do not recall if I was able to say anything else.

Four years later, I would return to clean out the house dad and mother built. He lived there for fifty years and one month before he spent his last two months in a nursing home.

This huge task me gave me a much needed opportunity to grieve for the pain and loss. This was a home I lived in for only one year as a senior in high school but returned to visit frequently over the years. My children and some of my grandchildren also visited there for such cele-brations as Dad's birthday or to go hunting or fishing with him.

While involved in this huge effort, I received help from two grand-daughters, their husbands, and friends and one grandson. In addition my friends Rose and Turra, and Jim Freer whose mother Edna was my dad's first employee. She worked for him for over thirty years until the business was sold. They all provided much necessary and appreciated assistance as everyone was helpful in so many different ways. Without all these volunteers I am con-vinced it would have been nearly impossible for me to complete this job alone.

Rose, God love her, invited all of us for supper whenever we were working at the house. It didn't matter if I had one helper or ten, everyone was welcome. I will never be able to repay her. Jim took care of so many details like the proper disposal of old garden chemicals. He often helped load my car for my return trip. He also checked on the house when I wasn't there and even showed the house to prospective buyers once or twice when I couldn't get back to do it. Turra, in spite of her allergies to cat hair (the house was full of it) went with me at least twice to clean and sort. She also drove my car on the last trip home while I manned a 17-foot rental truck filled with family heirlooms and possessions that I just refused to part with. A storm was headed our way and had already ice coated the roads at our final destination. I never got out of that truck until I arrived at my own front door. We did manage to avoid the storm. I had driven 30-foot box trucks in the past but that had been years before. Turns out, this ol' gal was still up to the challenge.

Eventually, after many months, all the stuff was gone, the grieving finished. I was ready and able to sell the property and move on. Now, I return once a year in May to plant flowers on the graves in the town cemetery just up over the hillside behind the house. I have now buried too many loved ones there.

CHAPTER V

SO UNEXPECTED

It doesn't interest me what planets are squaring your moon.
I want to know if you have touched the center of your own sorrow,
if you have been opened by life's betrayals or have become
shriveled
and closed from fear of further pain!
I want to know if you can sit with pain,
Mine or your own
without moving to hide it
or fade it, or fix it.
                                    Oriah Mt. Dreamer
                                    The Invitation

MICHAEL

Half way between the years of my father's death and the empty-
ing of his house, in 2006 my older son Michael died suddenly of
a heart attack at 45. He had many health issues but a heart problem was never recognized. I attribute this tragic event to the fact
that he was on a great deal of medication for pain as well as other
health problems. He also smoked heavily and drank too much
Mountain Dew. Michael just did not take good care of himself and
only seemed to find enjoyment when he came up from Georgia to
visit his children. He had three sons and four daughters and tried

his best after his divorce to keep them unified. With his passing it would all begin to fall apart. I tried as much as possible to pick up the pieces and be there for them.

At the time of his death I recorded in my journal:

I must make record at the end of this most painful week that my son, Michael, passed away of a heart attack. It has been a time of tears and laughter, of memories recounted by his kids; of steeling my own emotions in order to be strong for them. So much shock and sadness and sorrow and generosity and goodness has filled this week to such overflowing, it is still spilling out around us.

At his memorial service I chose to express the following:

> It has been said that we are all ordinary people living extraordinary lives. This life exists at the core of our being; it is the immutable and inexhaustible source that is both intelligence and love. We don't design it, we don't create it, we only get to express it or not. We are extraordinary because that is the way God created us. We can choose to live each day knowing that extraordinary things are possible for us and each of us is worthy to be assisted in the process.

> My son Michael chose to express himself in many extraordinary ways. He will be remembered by his children as a loving, caring dad who once took the runt of a cat's litter, named it Taz, fed it with a bottle and carried it around in his shirt pocket.

> His devotion to his children came through the endless miles he drove from Georgia to their homes

here in Pennsylvania. These past few years, he drove from Georgia to my home and then to Brookville, DuBois, Brockway, Oil City and Corry or Erie, so he could bring six of them back for various celebrations and weekend visits. Sometimes in the same day he would make the return trip. He came this distance frequently to celebrate birthdays and holidays, and to watch two of his daughters perform in 4H horse shows. Michael worked hard to stay involved in their lives and activities, despite being in a great deal of pain during all this time. Driving so many miles even four or five times a year made it more difficult. He kept an 800 number so any of them could call him when they needed to talk.

Michael was a loving son who tried to help me as much as he could when he was here. He was very knowledgeable about computers and would always get me updated. So many things come to mind about him. As a little boy, he was always tall for his age. Once he started to wear glasses, people called him "the professor" because he always looked so serious and usually carried a notebook. At a very young age he had such a deep voice that when he spoke, adults would look up to see who was speaking, only to discover they had to look down because the source was a little boy.

As the days and weeks stepped into place I continued to put some of my feelings into words as best I could. I have taken these from my journals.

The *§§* indicates journal entries made on different days.

§§

Suddenly the Universe says, "Sorry. Tilt," and it throws everything into turmoil. Once the dust settles, not much stands as it was and so you re-shuffle, hold on to the positive and give the rest to God. The tilt of that early morning phone call has shaken all of us to our core. We are working to re-balance, each in our own way. I pray we all manage it to the best of our abilities and move into a place of grace.

§§

I yearn to retreat into peace but there is always way too much to do; too many details to test one. Far too much controversy over "stuff" but that is the way of the human psyche when there has been such a lack of sufficient nurturing in lives. Doing the best I can to mediate.

§§

Yes, I am tired beyond tired. A weariness permeates my bones like nothing ever has before this happened. May it go away and never return. I never want to have to go through this ever again.

We will take his remains and place them in my family's cemetery plot. I am just grateful that there is space available beside Dad.

And so, Michael, my son, I know you are now free of pain and reunited with the souls, including my dad, who love and support you. Please know I love you and always have. I tried hard and failed often but did my best; please forgive my shortcomings. I'll do all I can to help these kids.

§§

And so it goes...life continues to move on despite our loss. The ebb and flow of daily things to do stays the course and therefore pushes us to do the same. It is lost energy to worry about the past. Surely I feel I could have done more for my son but those waters of circumstance have flowed beneath life's bridge, gone forever. All I have is now; each moment is precious. I pray to see the ways I can best use the time I have to help others and take care of my husband (who was becoming increasingly frail and now partially blind) and keep going with only love in my heart.

§§

How does one deal with the haunting questions and painful sadness? I surely feel I did not do nearly enough for him in his short lifetime. He could be so difficult to understand (diagnosed with Minimal Cerebral Dysfunction.) I only discovered years later while doing research for my under-graduate degree that the cause was due to too much anesthesia given me during the birthing process. He was born in the morning and I was still trying to come to at 5 p.m. in the afternoon. I love him but I do believe I failed him a lot. There is no way to repair any of it now. It is gone, it is done. I just have to find a way to live with myself.

§§

I want to strike out at everything and everybody and throw stones at the world. There are no words to describe my pain — **none.** *I know I'll come out the other side of this but I wish it could be tomorrow or Monday, at the latest. Just when I think*

I have learned some lessons and put them into practice, really living them, the Universe sends a curve ball that says, "Okay, try to catch this" This is one time I feel unable to muster the courage, fortitude and wisdom to be able to hold onto the threads that are left and weave my life together again. Yet, I know I must reach inward, outward and upward toward the light in order to be able to keep my sanity. Alone I cannot do it.

§§

I know deep in my heart, that all of us will continue to survive doing the things that must be done in our lives. But still there will be this hole, this empty space that nothing else will ever fill. The memories of Michael, son and father, will always remain. The painfulness of loss may slowly fade but the fabric of his life will remain steadfast in the hearts of those he touched.

§§

When my son died I reached out to all I knew as though I had a gaping wound and they could somehow staunch the flow of pain. Some responded with love and caring, comforting me in my terrible grief. Others turned aside, perhaps not knowing what to say or shielding themselves from the fear that such tragedy would rub off into their own lives.

I spent lonely mornings berating myself for all the things I hadn't done for my son, all the ways I had failed him. It didn't ease my pain. Yet, I knew down deep inside that somehow, this too would pass and I would be able to endure whatever I had to until I could overcome the sharp edges of this loss. A different person would emerge but I would persevere. I have. He is still with me in spirit. I wore his shirts around the house every day for an entire year.

§§

He has told me that his essence is well and happy. Frustration lingers because he is not able to influence his children more from where he is today. I'm not sure he could have endured, if still here, what some of them have been experiencing. I can only stand back and let them seek their means to better decisions, giving advice, lending a strong but soft shoulder, when sought.

Time moved on and so did I. Over the past seven years I have continued to be there for my grandchildren and now their children, as best I can. All but two live a couple of hours or more away from me. For years, trips like that seemed a piece of cake, but that cake is not nearly as inviting as it once was. Grandma is getting old!

CHAPTER VI

I'VE COME UNDONE

How moving is the sheer wonder of
being necessary to the life of another.
Howard Thurman
The Essential Writings

MILO, MY LOVE

My husband, Milo, the absolute love of my life, had been in failing health for several years. The year that my dad died, I actually was afraid I might lose this wonderful man, as well. However, he recovered some of his health but was no longer able to drive because he lost the sight in his right eye. As he became frailer he adjusted to his new limitations. Fortunately we were able to continue our quiet life together for several more years. In the end, a pair of falls that resulted in broken bones and hospital and nursing home stays in late 2010 and early 2011 resulted in too much loss of strength, vitality and mobility.

Deep inside I realized he was dying, but dying can take a very long time. I put my life on hold waiting for this transition. For the weariness I felt over the caretaking I needed to forgive myself. I felt stuck in place waiting for this circle to complete itself, knowing that the circle would be pulled in on itself soon enough.

By this time I understood that our time together was running out. Near the end of this journey, again from my journals:

§§

Where am I going? I feel stuck in time right now between his living and dying, holding my breath, trying to cling to whatever crumbs we have left; reluctant to let go, but not wishing for him to linger long in this chasm between life and death. On one hand, this is so painful emotionally to watch. On the other hand, it gives us time to say goodbye, which in too many instances these past few years has been denied me. I may not have always done everything right but I have tried my best to take care of him as his health and eyesight failed. He is now too weak to stand or walk. I do not believe he will make it back home a second time. This is not the way I planned it, but it is the reality of the situation.

Then, one morning when I went in to feed him breakfast, he said to me, "We have to have a long talk about life and death."

Once he had eaten and things were cleared away, I sat down on the bed and as we held hands he told me he felt his life just wasn't interesting anymore but that didn't mean he loved me any less. He related that he was so tired he just wasn't able to keep on going. I told him that the most important thing was that we knew we loved each other and that we were loved in return. After we talked, we hugged and then I lay down beside him and held him.

The end was coming so quickly at that point. I have read that your soul knows seven days before you pass that those days are all the time you have left. I have to believe, after our conversation, that he knew his end was indeed nearing. Within a day or two his lungs rapidly filled with fluid and he no longer was able to eat or drink. At some point on Saturday he just simply went to sleep and never regained consciousness. Fortunately his sons and daughter were also able to be at his bedside all weekend. On Monday before lunch, he passed away. I will never forget the feeling I had as I watched the pulse beat at the base of his throat until it ceased. It still is impossible to describe.

His son Bill told me that as he sat with his dad on Friday evening, Milo began to reach out into the air for something. When asked what he wanted or needed, his reply was, "I need to fix some loose boards."

When asked what boards and where, his response was, "The barn at the farm." This was the farm where he grew up. His brother Charlie's widow Eunice still lives there. After his funeral she told us that the barn had fallen down that very same night.

From my journal:

§§

Even when you know time is running out, you think you will still have more days to share with your loved one. But, the time is never enough, be it seconds, weeks or years. Every word could be your last although you don't realize it just then. My beloved is gone from me, turned over to the hands of the Lord. I know "my heart will go on" but it will never be the same without him.

On one hand I mourn, the tears falling often. On the other hand, I know I must build to the future, whatever it holds for me. The ache for his embrace may never disappear but I will have to learn to live without it. He is gone from me but I know he can see again and will experience all manner of great wonders.

Within a couple days of his passing, six wild turkeys appeared in the back yard and stayed awhile. I know he sent them to let me know he was okay, for only he and I understood the significance of the six. A number of years ago I could often count as many as two dozen wild turkeys gobbling and searching for food around the bird feeder. However, over the course of time, their numbers had dwindled to nothing and it had probably been two or three years since I had seen even one. Now, more than two years later, I have never spied another one behind or around the house. I have to believe that he will make his presence known in my life for a very long time to come.

His final resting place is among his family members who have gone on ahead of him. At his service I chose to say the following:

> Even when time is running out you think you will still have more time to share with your loved one. Yet the time left is never enough, be it seconds, weeks or years. Every hug, every word could be your last but you don't know it then.

> My beloved Milo is gone from me, turned over to the hands of the Lord and Charlie. I know Charlie is there beside him saying, "Welcome Little Brother, I've been waiting for you."

> There has never been anyone in my life quite like this gentle, loving, curious, extremely intelligent, yet unassuming man. He taught me patience among other things, but in a million years of trying, my

patience could never begin to equal his. He treated everyone the same, be you the floor sweeper or the president. He saw value in everyone and was always interested in hearing your "story". He maintained that even the fly on the wall knew something you didn't know...the sex of the flies around it.

We met nearly 18 years ago on my birthday in March, but that time was not nearly long enough for either of us. We danced around the issue of marriage for a long time. Finally, I was the one to propose and he was ready. We eloped! It saved a lot of fuss, much to the disappointment of his children (not to the marriage, just the method).

For many years I have said that he was the best person I could have ever welcomed into my life. He allowed me to be just exactly who I am, no holds barred. There was never any disapproval, any chiding over my ideas, feelings, beliefs. I tried to do the same for him. He was a night person, I am a morning person and so we often had to meet in the middle. Besides, real love is accepting the other for who they are, quirks and all, rather than trying to make them into your ideal partner.

He often told me of his parents and what helped their marriage. His father, John, said to his new wife, Lottie, "Lottie, there will be no jangling between us. If one of us is upset, the other will just leave them alone until they feel better." So, in our marriage and really, in our entire time together, disagreements were rare, but I could get run over by his engineer logic.

I told him, not long after I met him, I would rather have ten good years with him than twenty with anyone else I had ever known. Each year on my birthday, we would agree to try it again for another twelve months. We called it "renewing the contract". We got the really good ten years before his health and eyesight began to fail. My only regret is that I didn't ask for at least twice as much time.

He was a deeply caring, loving man and was truly loved by many in return. In the end the only thing that counts is the love you give away.

I knew late last week that he was getting ready to go. When I went in to feed him breakfast he said, "We need to have a long talk about life and death."

Over the course of the morning we did just that. He said he was too tired for life to be interesting any more. We assured each other of our mutual love and I told him that was the only thing that really mattered.

There is so much in life that gets elevated to a level far beyond its real importance. He was so keenly aware of this and was disturbed very little by the material matters of this world. Love is what really matters. In his memory, keep it central in your lives. Remember, love is God.

As the song goes, My heart will go on" but it will never be the same. Still, I am far richer for our time together. I don't regret one moment I had with him. I hope he felt the same.

But right now all I can do is muddle through.

My journal filled with almost daily notes on my grieving:

§§

It is not a new dawn just yet. The pain and sorrow still surround me. I try to allow myself whatever time I need to flow through this, knowing at some point I will get to the other side. I know he would not want me to be sad; don't believe he wants me to forget him either. How could I? We loved so much and shared such quiet together. We truly were lucky to have had the years together that we had. The thing I miss most is having his arms around me and I don't know if that longing will ever go away. I don't for one second regret lying beside him in the nursing home; just wish I had done it more. But, there always seem to be regrets and feelings of having not done enough. I have to overlook these. I am only human and did the best I could. I have to accept that, for I'm sure he did.

§§

And still the tears fall...probably will for a while. But the grief makes me old and tired and I don't want to feel that way. Just as with everything in life this too shall pass. Someday I will be on the other side of it.

It is good to be here quiet and not having to rush about. How I long to hug him and tell him I love him. I believe he still knows that.

§§

Grief...a brief moment of tears wraps around my morning thoughts as I struggle to deal with my losses. Yet, grief has stretched itself over so many years now, gathering strength with each new loss and then ebbing with time's passage, but never completely fading into nothingness. I feel it is a form of self-pity for I mourn for what I no longer have in my life. I should rejoice for the improvement bestowed upon my loved ones who have stepped to the other side. But alas, too often my view is so narrowly focused on myself.

I know I am moving through all this and it takes time. It is solely up to me to take the needed steps to continue what time I have left, in a positive way. It is okay to miss them and continue to love them. There will always be space in my heart for all that we shared, but I also want to build and reinforce the path that will lead me beyond the grief.

§§

I can see how my grief has already shifted in the past few weeks... it is not as raw, as wrenching. It is softer but still hangs heavy in my heart. Yes I will continue on, for there is no other choice. The grief will ease and life will be different, but life always is, day to day and year to year.

I know I'll be okay and I am accustomed to being alone. But it doesn't mean I miss him any less. How can I keep him alive in my heart? I am so afraid to let go of him. I know he will not magically reappear, alive and vital, like he did recently in my dreams. My grief is for myself and my empty arms.

54

The time we had passed so quickly while we were busy living it. That is as it should be. Did we take enough time to really appreciate each other? I hope so. I know I loved him and he truly was one, if not the greatest, gift I ever received.

§§

A year has now passed since my love drew his last earthly breath and still the tears fall. I miss him every day. I try as hard as I can to move on and put my focus elsewhere but there just seems to be a part of me that continues to long to feel his arms around me. Perhaps it will always be thus but only time will tell. I just have to deal with it as best I can, wipe the falling tears, move into each day with renewed hope and keep finding ways to deepen my passion in creating whatever I dare to create. I never want to lose the love that I still have for him but just simply find a place, a way to hold it in my heart until I see him again. I also hope that by leaning into what I do feel that it will help mellow it all out. Perhaps that will bring me to the point where I don't shed so many tears, and miss him so terribly. As the years fall away, it will surely be so. In the meantime, I must continue to move forward. I feel I shall have much work to do with all that every day will hold for me.

§§

From this day I move forward with perhaps a little more peace in my heart. I have to move forward because I cannot go back and I don't want to stay stuck. But it is in my nature to keep moving on, not often content to just be. Action and active are far more my style. I have survived this long year and have moved on in fits and starts, and I am still here. My heart may never be completely mended, but I can't focus on that and I have no way of knowing what the future holds in that department.

I do believe the years ahead will add new adventures for me to enjoy as well as challenge me. Life will be mostly what I make it, in so many ways. There will continue to be losses and ups and downs. I just pray I get more ups in the days I have left. I also realize these days are ticking down to the end. I really hope that my sand drips <u>very</u> slowly. I have so much I want to see and do and be. I am still able to see that life may provide the opportunity for some additional enjoyment. When I can't look for all that is good or I become too weary, then I will know I'm ready to cross the veil.

§§

Milo, my love, I miss you. I hope I will always miss you so that a part of you will still always be here with me. I'm doing okay and not too depressed most days now. I wish so much that you were here and we could go back and do the really good days again. Please watch over me, be my new guardian angel. I love you so! I know you are faring much better where you are and I am sure you are glad to be there. Please send me a sign now and then as the six turkeys were great.

§§

I miss him! I miss him! I miss him! Some days are better than others. I just want to feel him holding me, be able to put my arms around him. He was out of the house such a long time that his essence, his energy dissipated sooner than I would have liked.

The two weeks he was home during the holidays, his energy was so low that I believe it was not possible for it to remain and stay around me. There seems to be nothing of his I can touch and still feel him, except maybe the blanket I bought to keep him warm in the nursing home. However, I found I could not feel his energy, even there.

I could sit here and wish I had done a million things differently, but it won't bring him back; it won't buy us more time. To the best of my ability I tried always to be good to him. I can't have him back and I have to go on. I know he would not want me to be so sad. I'm sure he must be happy where he is and that there are all manner of things to delight his curious mind.

And, as the candle flame eventually burns down and goes out, life, as well, comes to an end.

§§

I just have to believe he is with me in spirit and will reveal his self to me. I wish he would come and talk to me. Maybe he is talking to me and I can't hear him. Perhaps it is too soon. Someday I will move beyond this sorrow.

Neither of us ever saw the time we had as limited; never saw the end coming until it was too late. Truly I am grateful for all the years we did have together, especially when his health was good and we could hike and go out to do different things. Unfortunately, the time together did not seem like it was long enough, but would a hundred years have seemed sufficient? Probably not, knowing what I know now. Will I wake up ten years down the road still wanting him? I miss his presence, his essence in this space so much.

§§

I cannot swamp myself with "coulda, shoulda". It serves no purpose. Life does not go on forever and we must learn to cherish what we have while it is in our hands. Most of the time I did, but there surely were times when I did not. Care giving is not an easy task nor is it my strong suit but I never stopped loving him. My absolutely greatest regret is that I did not hold him more. I truly believe now that it was his greatest need.

§§

I do love him but he is gone from me for now. Some day we will come together again. The earthly roles of our love that mattered so much to both of us are now simply gone and there is never a way to get that back. I will never feel him in my arms again. I knew it would come to this at some point, but still, I was unprepared. How can one ever be truly ready for the agony of such a loss? It seems to reach down into my very core. It will soften over time, but the present is filled with my tears and my empty arms.

§§

I will carve a new path for myself. I know he does not want his passing to hold me back. He would encourage me to live, just as he always did. He would especially like it that I have gone back to playing my beautiful drum that he gave me for a Christmas gift several years ago.

§§

I miss him but every day brings the feeling of a little more peace. That is as it should be. Yes, there is much to work through but I know it will come. It is okay for it is the natural ebb and flow of all living things but just harder to deal with when it hits so close to home. It is such a major loss to me, yet there is no way to go back and undo the regrets I have for not spending enough time in more loving ways with him. It can't be done. It was too easy to get caught up in the stress of all that was happening those last few years. I feel I just simply was not there enough for him. The loss to both of us cannot be measured and I am as sorry as I can be.

Life will go on because I am here. I know he would want me to feel that it is okay. He knew I loved him and I knew he loved me. What more can one ask?

§§

The time slips away so quickly that you wonder how it can already be tomorrow when it was only today. It all becomes a blur of events and people, blue skies and gray, tears and laughter. That last day waits quietly in the shadows. Even with awareness it can close the eyes with swift unexpectedness. The heart beat stops so quickly...one beat but not the next...the breath silenced forever. You can sit there, knowing it will happen; waiting for it. When it comes, you hate it with all your being because you do not want to let go of this presence that filled your life, that you have shared so much with. This includes all the joys and agonies, the laughter and tears of everyday living, and most of all, the love that tied you so tenderly together. The link remains but the physical manifestations are forever dissolved and that is the most encompassing *pain of all. Nothing can ever replace, in exactly the same way, what you shared with this other soul...**nothing**.*

But you have to go on and go on you do. Some day you will come out the other side of this dark tunnel, this overwhelming sadness and pain. No one can count the days. You can't even count them for yourself. They simply have no number. Hopefully, one day I will wake up and the sun will shine a little brighter and the tears will stream fewer and fewer. I know he is there and so much better off, but, oh, God, if I could just touch him again right now.

§§

What I wish for the most is to feel my Milo's arms around me again, yet I know that cannot happen. No amount of sorrow or pain can bring him back to me here. I feel now that there had to have been any number of times in those 18 years when he would have been more than willing to hold me and I was not. Payback? No, just simply life.

We so overlook the simple things in life that contain the real joy, the real meaning of what it is all about, because we allow the stress and distractions to overtake us. My regrets are really few and simply boil down to "I wish we had held each other more."

§§

Sometimes I feel like I've come undone, but then I knit myself back up so that I can somehow go on. I do believe my work here is not finished and I must continue. I fear nothing anymore. What lies ahead can never be as soul-rending as what I have already lived through, not even my own dying, and die I will, when my moment comes and my spirit travels home. For now, I remain bound to earth and living and trying to be of good use. I strive to understand the greater meaning of it all for I am always willing to share the learning with the hope I can get others to think about what is truly important.

We all have our own paths to walk; our own burdens and sorrows to weigh. On a tearstained sleepless night, I know in my heavy heart that nothing lasts forever, good or painful. Still, the losses and sorrows have dogged my days and nights, but not always anymore. Over time they are no longer my constant companions, but more like guests that still visit too often. Maybe someday they will forget where I live. For today I quietly struggle though these tears and move on into the light of a new dawn. Into the breaking, fresh day I strive to listen and learn and love and share what I have encountered. Hopefully it will help someone, somewhere to endure what life presents.

More than a year later, I still missed him, longed for him and sometimes the tears still fell. Even at the two-year mark I found the grieving continued but it has begun to turn more into a place of acceptance for where life currently holds me.

As I struggled through my early days of grieving for Milo, I had no realization that shortly things would become nearly over-whelming. The next major loss nearly crushed me.

After my son Michael passed away, the call coming in the middle of the night, I refused to continue to have a phone in my bedroom. I somehow thought that would prevent all future middle-of-the-night-calls filled with bad news. Oh my, was I wrong.

CHAPTER VII

BEYOND BELIEF

*Which has more value in your life,
where have you grown more and
learned more, where have you become more
wise, where have you learned patience,
understanding, equanimity, and forgiveness — in
your hard times, or the good ones?*
Ajahn Chah
Food For The Heart

DAVID

Less than three months after my husband passed away, I was awakened in the wee hours by a call from Sandy in Georgia telling me there had been a vehicle accident late the previous evening that had taken the life of my son, David. Sandy, his significant other, said he had rolled his truck over into a deep ditch while trying to help a friend move. It turned out that there was important information not given to me initially, but it would be revealed later.

The rest of the night was spent attempting to deal with the emotional turmoil of this terrible tragedy. My greatest concern was for his daughter, Haley, for I now would have to tell her that her dad was gone.

I waited until I thought she would be up and getting ready to leave for work. As the darkness gave way to a new dawn I called her and told her not to leave until I got there and talked to her. She only lived about 15 minutes away and so, before breakfast, I quickly went to break the devastating news.

When I told her what had happened, her only words were, "Now it will never be all right" and she sobbed and sobbed.

Despite my best efforts to keep them communicating, in the past few years their relationship had pretty much fallen apart. Somehow, neither of them could fully see the good, the positive in the other. Too much hurt drove the divide deeper.

It didn't seem possible that this nightmare could cut any deeper but it quickly pushed the blade in and twisted it. Once I returned to the house and began to call family and friends, I received another call from Sandy. The truth was that David had survived the accident, crawled out of the truck, talked to a couple of different men who stopped to offer help, climbed back into his truck and took his life.

How could this happen, I have asked myself again and again for a very long time. Why did I not see the signs of his desperation, sense that his life was going so badly? I know he told me several times he really needed to get out of there but I assumed that it was due more to lack of good work than his state of mind. Since we seldom missed a day without a phone call how could I not have known? For some of our questions there will never be any satisfactory answers.

Surely this last act was impulsive, a spur of the moment thing. No parent wants to ever deal with losing a child regardless of how it transpires. Circumstances such as these multiply the pain forever and I am certain I will still be trying to process the reasons to the very end of my days.

Because the state of Georgia does not recognize common law marriage, Sandy was powerless to claim David's remains. Being David's only child, Haley was considered legally to be the next of kin. We had to work quickly. I made the needed arrangements for papers to be signed and notarized, thus allowing me to pick up his remains and bring them back to Pennsylvania. I needed to get on my way for the long trip as soon as possible.

To have to later convey the real cause of death to Haley was gut wrenching for me. I didn't want to do it, but I also knew I would never want her to learn it from anyone else. After we went to the lawyer's office and signed the papers, I sat with Haley in her car and told her the bad news. We both cried again.

For a long time I have withheld the truth of what happened, because it is still almost impossible to talk about, even two years later. A very few close friends and his daughter knew from the beginning. There never in my life was a more difficult time to face reality.

This time I had to travel to Georgia to pick up his remains and deconstruct his life. The only other trip I had ever made there was when I went to sort out my older son's belongings and bring them back for his children.

Thankfully my first husband's niece, Karen, was staying with me at the time as she was in the process of moving to my area from Massachusetts. She courageously offered to accompany me. Alone, I don't believe I could have ever survived doing what had to be done. She was of such immeasurable help and above all, was very instrumental in my being able to maintain some level of sanity.

At that time I owned the property where David and Sandy were living and so everything had to be removed or disposed of and both buildings totally cleaned out. There would be no one coming back there to live. Sandy was in such bad shape she had to go into detox and so was no help at all in making any decisions.

By the time I was able to leave Georgia I knew I would never, ever return there myself. I will never be sure how I survived those two weeks but somehow I kept going until I was nearly coming undone. I couldn't wait to get back home and try to somehow glue myself back together.

Haley and I made all the arrangements for David's memorial service that would take place the Saturday following my return from Georgia. Since he had moved south seven years ago, it truly amazed me that so many of his friends and former co-workers came to talk with us before the service and share their stories. Friends from his high school days, including one from out-of-state, came to pay their respects. For his service the room was full.

I composed these words to read:

> Sometimes life is like a bowl of strawberries, all sweet and full of juicy goodness. Sometimes it is like a truckload of artichokes, thorny and tough. These past 21 days have definitely been great big artichoke days. But, once we get past the hard parts, there is plenty of sweetness. I know that someday soon, I will be able to move out of these dark shadows, back into the sunshine of life. I pray that all here who grieve can reclaim the joy and wonder that life has to offer.

Full of life and laughter, David enjoyed many things. He was creative, funny, courageous, helpful, caring and very hard working. Those who knew him can add to this list.

David was a loving, caring son who was always willing to help anyone he perceived as having a need. In fact, his last hours were spent helping a friend move his possessions out of his dream retirement home.

As a child growing up, he was adventurous and tried on many hats. I can still remember when he climbed so high in the apple tree I couldn't look. He did manage to get down on his own.

In junior high he played some football as well as the trumpet. He worked hard to look out for his older brother who just was never able to defend himself. David always said he had to live fast because he often claimed, even as he was growing up, that he was not going to live beyond his forties. He wanted to get it all in.

David really enjoyed hunting and fishing with my father who taught him a lot. Some of his most special memories were of those times. He had a great sense of humor which he needed if he was going to hang around my dad.

He was also an extremely hard worker. He came back two years ago to help with a lot of work on my house. When David said goodbye I had a strong feeling that I would never see him alive again. It was a feeling, a sense that I could not understand at the time, but never dwelled upon it or thought about it again until now. We usually talked every day, but I still missed him. I was really looking forward to the move that was to bring him to a new job closer to me.

David graduated from East Allegheny in 1981 and spent the next year at the University of Pittsburgh studying to be an engineer. Dropping out was a decision he always regretted. He then became an auto mechanic, but eventually was able to move into the building trades. He took a lot of pride in doing a good job for the people who hired him to build or remodel their homes and vacation homes. He proved to be a talented wood-worker and really enjoyed using Georgia mountain laurel in his designs. It was gratifying when I was in Georgia earlier this month and his friends told me how they respected him and thought so highly of him and his work.

He was a good son, always willing to help me. I'm sure David would tell you he moved me more often than he wanted to.

I know he loved his daughter but communication became difficult. Now he will never be able to appreciate what a special person she has become.

Lest I forget, he was an absolutely rabid Steelers fan. I happened to call him earlier this year right after a Sunday game started and when he answered the phone his first words were, "What are you, a Commie?" For several weeks after that, whenever I called, I greeted him with, "This is your Commie mother."

Just remember always what is placed on your plate is not nearly as important as what you do with it. Right now, this is one of those times I need to reach really deep to keep my universe from tipping upside down. I know God and my angels will keep me upright until I get to the other side of this.

This is a tragic loss for all of us who knew and cared about him.

Nearly as soon as I could absorb what happened, how his life really ended I knew my son felt he made a horrific mistake. There was no doubt in my mind that as soon as he took his life, he was pretty much saying, "Oh, sh%$#t, I shouldn't have done this."

Months later, when I finally got to talk to him in spirit, he confirmed my suspicions. He also told me that the major problem was that he just simply did not like himself well enough to change his life style. Thus, a life so full of promise was now gone.

Before summer ended we made the trip home to the family burial plot to place David's remains next to his brother, Michael. There was nothing more I could do. Now both of my sons were gone, reunited in the great beyond.

From my journals:

§§

What a long journey this has been and it's not over yet. Just to move myself through these days to get done what was needed has been such a huge challenge. Most of the stuff I brought back from Georgia has been sold, stored, given away, etc. Hopefully I can settle into getting my place shifted and changed into what and where I want to run my life from.

The pain of his passing is still present and I do need to take time to deal with it and clear it out. I need to take whatever time and energy this requires so that a day will dawn when this is all behind me and my sorrow is diminished to just a memory.

Being alone helps! So much commotion and to-do about everything is not favorable to establishing daily tranquility in my life. I need my peace, my quiet so that I can gather myself back up again and move into the creative space that I so desire. I still want to find myself going in a positive direction and be in love with life.

The tears have been so difficult to shed this time. I don't know if one can stuff the grief for such a long time that it becomes too late to open to the pain. I feel like that is what happened when Michael died. When Milo left me, I was determined that I would take time to work through my grief. Yes, I still miss him so much, but when David's passing broadsided me, that got put on hold as well. Now how can I best pick up all these broken pieces that can never be put back in the same pattern/ place in my life? How can I work through this grief and move on? I know that they are sending me love and that has helped to soften the edges of the pain and created some peace in my heart.

With David, my almost single regret is that I didn't realize how badly things were going for him personally. But, would my knowing have changed what happened? Doubt it. His free will put him where he was and allowed him to make his choices.

I hate it that these loved ones are gone from my earthly place, yet I am not anywhere near ready to join them. So, I have to redesign my inner space so that I can move on without them. How can I do this? I guess I just have to try to take tiny steps every day and pray to find peace knowing that they are all sending me love and supporting each other. Just now that seems to give me only a small measure of comfort.

§§

David, I still can't seem to really address you directly. It is so difficult to understand how you could have done this. It also saddens me so much that you felt such terrible desperation. I still don't feel able to talk with you and sense that you are not ready to tell me about it, either. I just hope that we can someday come to this conversation, so that I know that you are truly okay. Under the circumstances I feel it will take some more time. (It took eight and a half months before we were able to communicate through a third party).

My deepest, most identifiable pain and sorrow seem to be over my longing to be back in Milo's arms. Would it be because he was the strongest loving presence ever in my life?

§§

I wish I felt ready to talk with David but I can't quite manage it. I'm not angry, just sad that he felt he was so out of options. There is no way to change the events of these past months. I just have to gather up my courage and move on. I know I still have life to live and I really do want to do it. Perhaps that will be the only way

I can truly find my peace. I know I can go on but it seems to be taking a while to regain my balance.

§§

I am so thankful that spring has moved into summer and I can work outside. I seem to get the greatest satisfaction from creating beauty in the dirt. My hands do help me create my space and bring me peace.

§§

It is calmer now with much of the jumbled emotions and circumstances put aside or overcome. Life goes on, just differently, and I turn my attention back to the things I love and what I want to bring into my life.

Sorrow is still here but it is softer, less an agony than it was. I didn't break into pieces as I thought I might. I still miss Milo most of all, but he was my daily focus for so many years. He was my rock, my ocean of calm no matter how high the waves of life's troubles washed around me. Always, he was patient, loving, kind. I miss his loving arms most of all. Sometimes, especially in the middle of the night, I can still feel him snuggling me. But I feel guilty of my need for him and wonder if I hold him back from somewhere else he needs to be.

I do not seem to be able to open completely to the terrible pain of losing David. I do not feel able to talk with him yet and barely can stand to look directly at his picture that I have put with the others. I also truly believe he is not anywhere near ready to talk to me.

I ask that I receive some unmistakable sign when this conversation can take place. Hopefully, by then, I will be open to understanding what he has to say. The acute pain seems to have lessened so I am not certain if it is truly diminished or just stuffed deep inside.

§§

My grieving I know is not over yet and it well may never be... my losses are so indescribable! I still feel the pain and I may always experience it or it may just set up shop here for a long time. I cannot continue to suffer as much as I did while in Georgia for I feared I would crack. For now, I have managed to move into a place of awareness that seems to diminish the agony of these losses.

I miss my husband but my sons I miss in different ways and with a great deal of guilt attached. Why didn't I?????; endless rebukes to myself if I allow it. Still, they were both adults and made their own choices good and unfortunate.

The heart breaks but with prayer and loving support and being open to accept healing, it can mend again. No longer raw and cracked wide open I am also not yet fully healed. It will take more time, but I believe it can and will happen in the years I have left. I have faced these and other tragedies in my life. I pray that the worst is now past. Hopefully I can envelope myself in peace and healing.

§§

The sorrow of my losses, that I try to avoid, appears as tears on nearly a daily basis. Often they are silent tears, sliding down my cheeks unbidden. But they will have their way and crack open my heart even as I willingly open it to all the love that surrounds me as it is sent from the caring souls on both sides. Someday the pain will be gone but the love will remain, for that is all that truly matters. To purposely dwell forever in sorrow, to me, is a great error of living. I choose to move on with little steps each day that hold the door open to living in peace and love.

§§

What an uneven path this grieving is. There are lots of days when if I don't think too hard about the losses, I am okay and can go about other things. There are days when it is so in my face that all control is lost. There are also times when the tears flow without much thought of any of it. My best defense seems to have become to keep busy outside and leave all the painful reminders in the house. So I ease into the flow of recreating myself, as so many of my old defining boundaries of wife, caretaker, mother, are erased. Now I must make a new life and hopefully redefine what 75 looks like. I will make an effort to carve out a new path to encourage others to follow so that they can also create a new song in their own hearts.

Joy is mine to reclaim on a daily basis. Some days I grab the joy and laughter. Other times I leave it under the covers when I rise. There are moments when it escapes my grasp halfway through my waking hours and I have to rediscover it like a pin lost in the carpet. But I know it is always there waiting for me, just as the grief is.

Dawns arrive when I can easily make the choice for joy. It is still possible to get mowed down by the depths of my pain. Questioning the length and depth of the process is useless for there is no perfect answer. Quite simply, when it is done, it will be done. It is impossible to set a deadline or completion date because for grief they do not exist. Life will continue in joy and sorrow. I choose joy as much as I can and simply weep through the days when grief will not be subdued. My dedicated choice is to keep going and create a new life.

§§

Am becoming more at peace every day...start by opening my heart to all the love that is being sent to me. That love matters a great deal and really helps me wash away the sorrow. I know these loved ones are with me in spirit and will help me through this grieving. I am happy that they are together on the other side, healthy and making peace with themselves.

Love is truly the only thing that matters and what we give away (unconditional love) will come back to us, just as I feel it coming back to me. Love is what sustains us when life produces the inevitable pain that simply is a part of the whole. But our pain is only portion of life. If we allow it to consume us, we permit it to have mastery over us...it then runs our life. Grieving is a normal reaction to the loss of a loved one. We need to remember, we grieve because we have lost. They have moved into another dimension where they are whole and healthy again. Do we want to deny that opportunity to them? Not I. Therefore, I have to open my heart every day to the love that they are sending me, knowing I did the best I could in my earth relationship with them and simply let the rest go.

We are imperfect human beings. If we were so perfect we would no longer dwell in this place. While we are here we still have work to do. My intention is to keep on living and doing that which gives me joy. This includes loving others and accepting them for who they are...simply other imperfect souls...struggling to make it through this lifetime and needing all the love that I and others can give them.

The grieving continued and still does, but the passage of time and keeping myself very busy with various projects has helped. There actually is a great deal more in my journals I wrote as I wound through the days. However, I feel I have included enough, if not perhaps too much, to chart my course along this path that nobody ever wants to walk. I feel that what I have written here demonstrates how these experiences have reshaped me into a stronger, less willing to tolerate nonsense, more focused on the positive, person that I now am.

For me, I'm at the short end of life's stick and just know that the time truly is now or never to do what I most want to do. Thus, as I continue to grieve for these painful losses, I am, indeed, moving on into a life that includes lots of fun and laughter. More than ever I am dedicated to doing what most makes my heart sing.

Regardless of what the Universe has in store for me or what gates of fire I have already passed through, I have found I can survive and survive I will. What choice do I have?

To this day I am still working to absorb all the losses and especially David's death. Even though I communicated with him more than a year ago, I'm not totally able to move on as much as I would like. Still, I am getting better about all of it. To say I still miss my husband is an understatement, but I am at peace with his passing. I do know that they are around me and send me their love. As well, they seem to send me a little help now and then with a crossword puzzle or a computer glitch!

CHAPTER VIII

CHOICES! WHAT CHOICES?

I learn by going,
where I have to go.
Theodore Roethke
The Waking

So many people tell me that they will never understand how I made it through all that happened in 2011. Oh! I do not recall being offered a choice. Surely if I had had the opportunity to keep my husband around, well and sighted that is, I would have been more than happy to do so. I would love to still be hiking the Laurel Highlands trails and enjoying all the other things we shared. Ditto with both of my sons, as well as my father; I would be delighted to still have all of them in my life. If possible, I would never have gone through such trauma as a horrendous house fire either. I can think of a few more things I would have been happy to have avoided in the past. Who knows what other great surprises the Universe still has in store for me?

Many, including me, believe that before we came to this earthly place, we selected the lessons we wanted to experience. It is also possible that those people we have a relationship with here are some of the souls from our group in the other dimension. We all agreed to help one another with the struggles we chose for this current life. I have sensed that over the course of my lifetime I have established relationships with people who, early on, I felt a deeper sense of connection with than I did others. These are the friends with whom I have formed my deepest and closest bonds. Is it what some consider unfinished business or we are simply here to support one another? I suppose it could be both.

When I look around, I sometimes see individuals who become so traumatized by an event that they remain forever in the grips of whatever it was that turned their lives upside down. Others mourn the future while their loved one is still here, moaning and fretting about what they think will happen. Some withdraw, particularly following the death of a loved one, as if they somehow believe that that is what is expected of them and Heaven forbid, we wouldn't want people to talk.

Often those who have been married for the greatest part of their lives and lose their spouse, really don't know how to go on without the other half. After sharing the majority of a lifetime with that special someone, it must feel as if an actual body part has been severed. It has to be far more difficult than the loss I endured. After all, Milo and I didn't even get to scoop out twenty years, never mind fifty or sixty.

Perhaps I have fared better than many because there seems to have always been a part of me that I kept for myself. It could be viewed as being selfish. But it seems to be just the bent of my independent Aries personality coupled with the effort to save something of myself when so much else went awry across all the years of my life.

So no, no one asked me if I wanted to opt out of the losses and tragedies. I just picked up the load and did what had to be done. Most people do.

Regardless of what the future holds, I have no doubt that I will weather it as well as I can. I have already come this far and it is way too late for me to quit. Besides, what good would it do? Nothing can be reversed, done over or undone. The only viable thing we can do with the past is to right any wrongs, if at all possible and chalk the rest up to experience we must have needed.

I have always maintained that life isn't fair, because it really isn't. Once you can move beyond that fact you will manage to do what needs to be done. Believe me, at every turn there is guidance and comfort to be found by turning to God in prayer and asking for all the heavenly assistance that you need. At times you may have to listen really, really hard, and perhaps it will take time and practice to absorb it, but the comfort and wisdom are there.

I finally learned I could only do my best by working on the things that I can control. This does not include trying to control other people. It took me a long time to understand at gut level that I could not change the events in the lives of my sons and grandchildren. No amount of money, talking, or pleading could solve their problems. If they could not see the necessity of change, or were not willing themselves to make what I saw as better choices, it was not my responsibility. Besides, what I thought was the answer might not necessarily be the answer for them! Heart-breaking yes, because we always want the best for our offspring and their children. We really want them all to succeed, to find their real place in life. The absolute truth is that each of us must carve out our own path as adults. Too much help, too much assistance and we end up treading water endlessly. Everyone needs to choose their own options, find their own answers.

Here is where the real choices lie. We face opportunities, time and again to make changes that can have a profound effect on our lives and our futures. With enough wisdom and knowledge gained through living we learn to make better choices. Keep working at it because this choice making, as I see it, will never be over until we cross that final bridge.

Life's challenges are never ending, twisting and turning our lives upside down sometimes. As is so often said...it matters not what life hands you. What is important are the choices you make with the events that appear, especially those unbidden. There are times we can only slosh through it all, up to our armpits, navigating with little direction. If we manage to keep going, eventually we will find that the sun is still shining and life turns brighter and a little easier once again.

In reality it is all so fleeting. None of it goes with us except what we carry in our hearts as opposed to what we carry in our pockets. I have yet to see a moving van behind anyone's hearse!

What are you carrying in your heart today? Love, light, and laughter or is there anger and hate? You may not be able to see that there is love available to you from an earthly source, but there are other options. God is always available and always loving. Learn to reach out in prayer and don't be too timid to ask to be shown the love you need. It may not happen all at once, but every day pay attention long enough to start the flow of love moving through your heart. One day you will realize that the sadness that surrounded all the dark things has melted away and light and love fill your life. Love is all that matters anyway.

You do have choices you can make about how you will manage your days and your energies. No, it is not always easy, but it is easier to make conscious choices if we don't allow ourselves to get mired in all the drama around us.

Daily choices color my waking hours. Where each day takes me will depend upon my thoughts and where I direct them. Think "sad" be sad. Think "lonely" and my day will be filled with loneliness. However, if I think "love" I will be inspired to act with love. I enjoy thinking "peace" for I so love to dwell in its place. When I think "thankful" I am able to wrap myself in a blanket of life's gifts. As I dwell on what kind of person I truly desire to be and what is really necessary to have, all else falls away. Could your life be different if you made more positive choices?

I personally know an elderly lady, in her nineties, who sits alone in her beautifully furnished apartment in an expensive retirement home, unable to understand why everyone she is connected to doesn't wait in readiness to fulfill her daily whims. She has family nearby that now includes a great-great-grandchild. This family is composed of compassionate, caring, loving individuals who are as helpful as they can possibly be.

Why is there such a problem? This matriarch has made choices across her years that have put her, just like the rest of us, right where she sits today. Years of being petty, disdainful toward others, arrogant about how much better her truckload of toys is and how superior the circumstances are that she has experienced, have left her with an empty heart and empty hours and she just doesn't understand why. Her family continues to help her as best they can and include her in family celebrations and other events but they tire of her tirades and self-absorption. All the money and grand possessions in the world do not buy love and compassion. Again, choices are all important, through every step of our lives.

As a rule, none of us reach out to help and care for others with of what we might receive in return. We just do what we do as part of our caring human nature. We all know others who really go the extra mile for someone or some cause. They truly have no concern for whether or not the light will shine on them for what they have done. Their concern is not for themselves. They have made the choice to do what stirs their heart into action. I do believe that is all that God asks of any of us...make choices that will help some-one around you: love the unlovable, forgive the unforgivable. Your soul will benefit more than you can know even while you hold this earthly space.

CHAPTER IX

THE BIG "F"

Holding on to anger is like
grasping a hot coal
with the intent of throwing it
at someone else;
you are the one who gets burned.
Buddha

It is big and it is difficult, for the "F" stands for forgiveness. It is something that I have faced often enough throughout my days, and I know of no lives unaffected by it. Forgiveness is a fact of life that flows strongly as an undercurrent through the center of life. We can be looking for forgiveness from someone else, as well as from ourselves, without even realizing it. We can deny or offer this gift to others. Sometimes there is nothing to be forgiven.

What is it about this quality of life issue, this facet of our deepest sense of well-being that is so strong, that makes forgiveness so important to us? Is it those words, the admonitions from the *Holy Bible* that echo within our consciousness regarding right and wrong? Is it some inherent instinct that we carry within? Perhaps it is a deeper self-whispering that working toward an eternal state of forgiveness would help us make peace with ourselves.

Whatever it is, it can come easily or tie us into knots for a lifetime. Unforgiveness fills us with resentment and pain until we end up bitter and lost, forgetting that a choice existed.

For most of us, the main issue we forget regarding forgiveness is that we have already been forgiven for everything by the most important presence that will ever exist in our lives, here as well as on the other side. God has already granted us forgiveness. We must learn to accept what has already been given for the gift that it is meant to be.

The first major issue regarding forgiveness I can remember facing me was with my mother and the relationship I longed to have with her. As I grew into my teen years I knew that serious problems existed in our family. I also became more aware of the deep inadequacy I felt because I saw her as not nurturing or loving me. Regardless of what I did or didn't do, why couldn't I ever receive her approval, her attention, her love? It seemed to me that my older brother had no trouble getting plenty of both. I felt that I could do ten things right and she would always find the one I left out. Somehow I was always short of where she seemed to think I needed to be.

I began to resent her addiction to alcohol and the negative effects it had on the entire family on a daily basis. It also made me ashamed of her. Asking my teenage friends to come home with me after school was no longer possible. Nearly every day, I dragged my feet in every imaginable way to keep myself away from the house for as long as I could, for she drank constantly. I just felt so lost, so unloved and unnurtured and I began to adopt a victim persona, i.e., I couldn't do things because my mother was an alcoholic. After just a few years of this track, thankfully, someone told me to just get over it. I worked at it, but the residual effects of our inadequate relationship remained even after her death.

As I matured, I began to take a more realistic look at my mother and her life. She grew up the oldest in a family of four girls and two boys. Her father was an alcoholic. Her mother was pressed to work to feed the family when most mothers stayed home to care for their children. I can actually remember my grand-mother during WWII, sewing parachutes in a factory in Buffalo, New York. She always was an excellent seamstress and continued to sew for others until she was nearly ninety.

My mother never talked much about her childhood, but I have to assume it included heavy responsibility for all those younger siblings. She did mention, at one time, how difficult it was for her to hold onto her own possessions because her sisters were always "borrowing" them. Being pressed at a young age into household duties and caregiving would have meant it was no childhood at all.

In addition, my mother married very young and had my older brother barely a month after her seventeenth birthday. I arrived two years later and my younger brother came on the scene in another two years. A difficult aspect was that both my father and his mother simply had very strong personalities and that greatly influenced everything. Especially at 17, and even in later years, any small glimmer of who she might want to be was quickly buried under an avalanche of all that was expected to be properly done.

The one factor that we did share was rejection. I always felt rejected by nearly everyone to whom I was connected. Because of her addiction it was obvious to me that she felt she was rejected by her family. I saw evidence of this disdain in their behavior toward her. The irony was that all but one of her siblings suffered from problems with alcohol addiction during their lives.

Eventually, I came to realize that my mother, no doubt, did the best that she could with the cards that she was dealt, just as we all do. It seemed sad that she never really had any idea of who she was or perhaps what her real talents were. Long ago I forgave her for the anguish that I suffered all those years. My life has been so much richer than hers how could I not? This forgiveness freed me from the sadness and hurt I had clung to and I moved on to a better place emotionally. Still, when she died, I grieved terribly for what was never to be mine. I knew, more deeply than ever, that now it never would be possible. The little girl inside me had no choice but to grow up and move on.

Nearly 23 years later I would hear my granddaughter sob, "Now it will never be all right," when her dad died. How well I understood her pain.

I have never been a person that held grudges or kept hard feelings holed up for long periods of time. Usually I manage to just blow small incidents off and continue living without rancor. More able than many, I long ago adopted an attitude of allowing others to make their own choices. I have never been a controlling person. Time would, however, pull me into a place of such magnitude of misdeeds by others that, at that moment, there was simply no forgiveness I could muster initially.

I could never have envisioned any of these events as a possibility in my life because my father was always a man of his word and I had been raised on the tenets of honesty and hard work, etc. When my father passed away, I found that his estate/my inheritance had been raped, pure and simple. Also, family heirlooms were taken by others and there was no hope of recovery. Because of the process used and the really bad legal advice I received, there was no way I could change anything.

It took me months to work through all of the shock, resentment and indignation. Finally I realized the resentment was keeping me awake too often in the middle of the night and affecting my health. I had to release all of it. I knew it was not what my father had intended. Actually, the first time I contacted him on the other side, he advised me not to be mad at anyone. I needed to take him at his word but it would require some very conscious work on my part to release all of it. Finally I was able to let it go. I learned to say, "Help me to forgive everyone for everything" on a daily basis and that began to move me through the process. What freedom I felt to be able to do this so that I no longer had this overwhelming burden weighing down my life.

Forgiveness was not yet finished with me as another really big challenge would mushroom over the horizon of my life. This one would prove to be the most difficult. For years I had maneuvered through the ups and downs of my son David's addictions to alcohol and sometimes, drugs. He was so bright, so personable and had so much potential buried inside. Why couldn't he overcome these problems?

After his daughter Haley was born, I begged him to not do to her what my mother had done to me. He stopped drinking for a month or two and then went back to his old ways, telling me that he could not see what difference being sober was making in his life. A life, where at that point he was only half the problem, as Haley's mother was dealing with her own addictions.

Perhaps he was simply too much like his alcoholic father. He did tell me, after all was finished with his earthly life, that the major dilemma was that he just didn't like himself enough to make the necessary changes. Naturally his lifestyle led him to become involved with another woman immersed in the same addictions as he had. I cannot help but believe that a more positive influence could have turned him around, but it was not to be.

After he took his own life, I was so full of resentment and anger as well as all the pain and sorrow, that I could not think rationally about David, Sandy and their life together, crippled as it was with the addictions. I hated it that he was gone and truthfully, I did blame her for what part I felt she played in the destruction of his life. If only!!?? If only!!?? But what was the point?

In the beginning I could only focus on just getting through each day. I didn't even care then, if I could move to forgiveness. It wasn't as important as my sanity! As I look back, I now know that I created pain in the lives of others due to my omissions and oversights and my one-sided focus. As time moved on and the pain eased, it became obvious to me that I could not hold on to this terrible agony that was so unlike me, forever. I simply had to release it, let it go. It was not accomplishing anything and only added to my emotional burdens. I renewed my efforts on a daily basis to "forgive everyone for everything including myself" as I worked diligently and consciously to move forward. I renewed contact with Sandy in hopes that this would help us heal. I believe that it has been a good decision for both of us.

So often I have talked with people who just don't seem to understand the value of forgiveness. It has been said that holding back, refusing to forgive only hurts the unforgiving. The object of your anger and hate usually is ignorant of your mindset and they continue to live their life as they please. Your unforgiving attitude only hurts you in the end, hiding like a cancer inside, eating you away. Why would you willingly do this to yourself?

Oh, but here we go again...life isn't fair, you say. Why should you let them get away with what they have done? They should suffer for their misdeeds! Well, to work backwards through these points: in the *Holy Bible* it is written that vengeance belongs to God, not to us so why not let them get away with whatever? What they send out may come back to visit them, sometimes in spades. I know you can hardly wait. Again I repeat, life isn't fair, so get over it and move on.

It seems entirely probable we get so upset and hurt by others because we tend to think that whatever happens is all about us. What about whoever did this dastardly deed to you? Did you ever stop to think that it is nearly impossible, no matter how well you know someone else, to figure out what is in their head or how their mind works? It never will be on our radar screen. We assume that what they did applies directly to us, without any real knowledge of what might have triggered their behavior. In fact, it is not necessarily about us. Truly I believe that there are only a few individuals in this world who act with deliberate meanness or a conscious desire to hurt others. Most of the harmful behavior around us seems to stem from greed or an inability to practice self-control. In addition, the bizarre attitudes induced by addictions to drugs and alcohol, and too often anymore, mental illness need to be added to the mix.

I cannot stress enough the importance of understanding that you really do have the ability to change what you think about and hold in your thoughts at any given moment. It is possible to turn your thinking processes into a constructive mechanism rather than a destructive tool that holds you hostage. It does take awareness, effort and patience. There is no way it's a McDonald's drive-through, instant process.

First, try to be aware of what you are actually thinking. Examine what it does to your mood and your day. Everything starts with this awareness. Write down the thoughts that you are able to capture for just a few minutes over the course of a few days. Awareness is the absolute key to all of it. You will never be able to fully grasp every thought you have, for so many are too fleeting. If you only can take ten minutes out of your day to start with, it will help. Just try to get the general drift of where your mind takes you. It may be to places of unrest, anger, sadness or some other negative state. Perhaps you can see the good in where your day takes you. Once you have established a pattern to your thoughts, with special emphasis on weeding out any negative ones, decide what you are going to replace them with. Again, this step will take time, patience and real awareness on your part to do the work but it will change your life for the better. You can actually influence those around you by having more positive thoughts govern your days.

Remember when I had a house fire, and I decided I could not let the tragedy defeat me? I made a very conscious decision to make "I will not let this defeat me" my mantra for a long time. Back then I did not realize it might have been better to turn the statement into a more positive one. Perhaps "This fire will open new and better doors in our lives," or "We are all grateful to be alive and moving in a positive direction" would have been better. It actually did not seem to matter so much what the actual words were at that time. The motivation provided by the ones I used aided in keeping me somehow moving forward, although at times it was in fits and starts.

When I was so deeply troubled by the events regarding my father's estate and the resulting negative thoughts, I chose to say to myself, "Don't go there; just don't go there." This would stop the negative reactions in mid-thought. Eventually, I was able to avoid them completely. A quick response dissolved the thoughts before they could take hold in my mind. A large percentage of people would not even consider this process possible. Maybe they just like to wallow around in whatever particular mud puddle they call home, preferring to be a helpless victim or just plain lost. Many people probably have never even thought about controlling a part of their mind that they have always allowed to just run wild over the hills and valleys of life. I actually have talked to others who believe that there is no way to control their thoughts.

Please believe me, for it is possible to change your thought processes and move into a more positive place so that you can open to all the greater good the Universe has to offer. I am living proof! Try it, you'll like it!!!

Forgiveness is always an option for all of us. As I have worked to practice it in my life, it has opened new doors to my emotional health.

Two instances stand out in my mind that have absolutely required more forgiveness on the part of others than I could ever imagine. One is the father/husband in the New England area who forgave the killers of his wife and daughters. The other is the man who forgave his own son for killing his wife and daughter, who were also the son's mother and sister. These situations have required forgive-ness on a level far above what would ever be faced by most of us. There are many more examples around the world where others, lives profoundly changed by major tragedies, seemingly unforgivable acts, have found the courage and the fortitude to step forward and do what we are all admonished to do...love the unlovable and forgive the unforgivable. Presented with similar situations I really am not certain I could ever find room in my heart to make such a move. These two men, and so many others, represent the real face of forgiveness.

There is a lot more that might be said here about forgiveness. I could go on for pages, offering others' words up to your eyes. But

I can only give you what I have grown in my own heart, for that is where I have reached my deep understanding of what the important act of forgiveness means on the most personal level. All that pain and anguish that we bring into our lives spreads to all around us when we fail to forgive and is simply not worth the price we pay. From the most heartfelt sense of my being, I implore everyone to please bring yourself to the point where you can forgive yourself and all others that you hold locked in this prison. Run the hot water of love over that terrible lumped up heap of despair that you hold onto like it was gold and let it melt down the drain of forgiveness never to be brought back to life. You will never regret it and your life will improve so immensely, you will be amazed.

CHAPTER X

GRANDMA GURU

*The purpose of our lives is to develop
our souls and to spread the light
of heart and spirit far and wide.*
                    Dr. Judith Orloff
                    Emotional Freedom

For so many years I was always in such a rush to get to some place better than where I thought I was in the moment, never satisfied. Surely, I believed, that around that upcoming curve, over the suddenly appearing hurdle, or jumping off the next mountain I would find the treasure of happiness and peace I sought. In fact, several years ago I penned the following note to myself:

Yes, I really do need to learn to live in the "now" of each day. I have always rushed through my days reaching for some future insight that would reveal my true purpose. Maybe it is just simply to understand, enjoy and fully appreciate the present. Always I have sought the solution down the road, but it may be that it is here, each and every day. Just as I take time each morning for my quiet moments, I need to carve out time the rest of the day to see what I can do for my fellow man, enjoy Milo's company and the sound of the voices of those I love when I visit with them on the phone. I need to learn to also delight in the changes in nature as

I pass them along the road. Just maybe, the act of slowing down will provide me with deeper insight. On the other hand, maybe simply learning to live in the now will be the greatest insight I will ever need.

It is life changing to recognize that the Universe knows what it is doing and it does it all in Its own good time Even at this late date, I can't be more certain than anyone else about what the future holds. I just have to be willing to feel my way along and do what is best each day. For years I floundered around, darting here and there, trying all manner of things. I was afraid of never finding my "aha" moment, deeply worried that my life would be wasted. Now I worry less and accept that life flows for each of us just as it should.

What has happened to the days and ways of living that had a rhythm to it, a pace that left time for lying in the grass to search the clouds for the secret pictures they held...explore more quietly what the world had to offer? Did it ever really exist or do I just think so?

The quiet world is still here but all its occupants seem to be on fast forward like a VCR tape. All the new technology that includes cell phones, smart phones, Ipads, computers and other gadgets are wonderful in their place. They serve many useful purposes in this world. These innovations are also difficult to get away from. Because of the convenience and constant connection, we are implored to do more, better, faster, while staying in constant contact. People become increasingly stressed as all these new innovations create tremendous pressure that is difficult to get away from.

I have always been quick to move to do what needed to be done. For all of my adult years I have said that once my feet hit the floor each morning, I was moving. I had friends who called me their "Energizer Bunny." I still move in the mornings, but not nearly as fast. Recent years have found me practicing and fine tuning the ancient arts of being still and quiet and contemplating on both of these treasures.

In truth, I see now that I found the seeds of this quieter life style just living with Milo. Believe me that man was never in a hurry for anything or anyone. I know it was not a word he ever used. He did, however, know how to be still and quiet. It all seemed an ingrained part of his nature. Perhaps I took it up a step or two as I was interested in understanding it in a deeper way. He was content to just be without all the examination. It could be also, that he already understood it in some innate way.

Taking morning time for myself I began to understand that a vault of valuable knowledge was opening for me. So many, with so much on their plates could consider this self-indulgence a terrible waste of time. I came to view it as another gift that the Universe granted me.

The rewards I gain from sitting in my "quiet morning place" as I sometimes call it, have blossomed. For one thing, I find I have a greater ability to remain calm in the midst of the world's dramas. In addition, I feel more centered and focused throughout the day. This beginning definitely sets the tone for all that follows. I have more patience with almost everything and everyone, including myself; and it has held me up through all that I have had to embrace.

Each day is all that we have. I know it may seem that I have repeated this idea too often. Still, it is the honest truth but far too easy to ignore. We always think we will pay better or more attention to tomorrow or the next day. How many of those that woke yesterday but not today ever thought that would be the last daylight they would ever see here? Unless they were seriously ill, I doubt that any of them even considered the possibility. No one else ever wants to think that on a daily basis either. It is better to just be so grateful for what appears on our plate. Each day is the only one we have. Hopefully, with awareness we will rejoice in it and make good use of it.

For so long I couldn't seem to find my way, but slowing down has opened me to what was there all along, gliding just below the surface of my being. I do believe that I still have much learning to do and it will come as the Universe understands that I am open to it. My life does not appear to be an unproductive failure as I once thought. I now realize that even the small daily tasks I perform, when done with love and kindness, light the path to a life filled with meaning.

I am learning to honor more consciously the natural rhythm of the ebb and flow of all my days that always ran just outside my awareness. There will be, as always has been, birth and death. We all come and go and new souls move in to fill the empty spaces. The seasons change into new, yet familiar colors. The tide moves in on new breezes each day. The sun comes up somewhere every morning to announce the dawn. This gives each of us the opportunity to renew our efforts at living the thoughtful, conscious life.

It is good to remember to be present each day in everything we say and do. Only by living in a meaningful manner can any of us set the example for others. Each person has to walk their own path and they may never be able to move beyond the complex webs that they weave. Unable to untangle what others choose to design, I can only live and walk my own path of love and compassion. Hopefully the light of promise shines bright enough for everyone, on the chance that they may notice and turn toward it in the process of learning more about the purpose of their lives.

Life can be exciting, but only if we are truly willing to examine the possibilities. We need to stay open to inspiration provided by the voice within. Sometimes it is difficult to listen because we get so busy maintaining the selves we present to the world.

There is much to be said for the ordinariness of life. It gives us routine and provides some measure of meaning to our lives. It also grants us small opportunities to help others in need of love, encouragement, kind words and many of the other things that could light their days. Grand gestures may not always be needed or even count for more, if one is keeping score. It is the little things that generally vex us. It is also the little things that give us some measure of hope for ourselves and for others.

We need to remember that for every loss there is a gain. Every start means a finish somewhere down the path. Any new beginning eventually ages and ends. I was born and I will die, as will everyone. Doors open and as they close, new ones appear, ready for our unlocking to explore the next opportunity. Even a jar of peanut butter has a limited existence; eventually someone takes the last knife full! Nothing is ever static. It all constantly changes, just as the grass grows and young become old, given the chance.

As the years pass, it becomes more important than ever to learn to integrate the losses of life into our daily existence. We must grow to accept that dying is part of our lives. Otherwise, too much energy is spent burying the losses. What once was can drain us of energy to recognize what life still has to offer.

Everyone I know dislikes change and as we age, we become more ingrained in the "status quo." The same old, same old is our comfort zone and we would rather reside right there, thank you. Anything that disappears from our presence drags us, kicking and screaming, into a void that simply requires, by nature, a replacement. Some of us will choose to fill it with hope and inquisitiveness. Others will opt to cram it full of dread, bitterness and even addictions. Abandoning healthy choices only makes our losses etch deeper.

Life is so short how can we justify wasting it? Maybe when we were younger and so full of ourselves, viewing ourselves as invincible, we really believed that all would go on forever. We somehow assumed things would remain just they were or at the very least, another chance would always appear on our horizon. So, lost opportunity did not seem so important. As we move forward through the years the impact of it all becomes more profound. Now the questions can center on, "How much more time will I be granted?" "Is there any real value in anything I have done so far?" Even, if we are truthful with ourselves, "Do I need to make amends for anything I have done or said in the past or perhaps as recently as yesterday or today?" It all dwindles down to what time we might have left and how to make the best use of what is uniquely ours to offer.

As I began to heal from the surgeries and the two initial losses I desired to work more on moving into a new place within me that would fit who I had now become. I continued to have the willingness to grow more spiritually. I asked whether I could seize enough understanding to justify what the Universe offered me. Who could say what would be enough? Would it be enough to be a caregiver, especially when I became resentful at times; or could that be, in and of itself, a years-long lesson, one that would push me to look more outside myself and not be so focused on what I wanted to do? It is difficult to say, for life presents itself in different colors on a daily basis. Still, my desire to progress often simply got lost, swallowed by the daily mundane. I worked to move into the frame of mind that I was indeed blooming right where I was, for it was not necessarily up to me at that point where I got to shine my light.

Regardless of what the future holds, I have no doubt that I will weather it as well as I can. I have already come this far and it is way too late for me to quit. Besides, what good would it do? Nothing can be reversed, done over or undone. The only viable thing we can do with the past is to right any wrongs, if at all possible and chalk the rest up to experience we must have needed.

These days I continue to work to absorb the information, the learning, the lessons that appear along my way. I am delighted to be just exactly where I am these days and pray I will be able to continue for at least a few more years. I would prefer not to outlive my usefulness or my money. I still would like to get some more interesting living fitted into the days that continue to show up on my calendar.

As so often happens, more so than in the past, the losses seem to come closer together. The world is not that big oyster that you can keep plucking pearls from anymore; the gems, as the years, are fewer, life narrows. Still, there are ways to blossom, stretch and grow until even the end can present a final opportunity for one last spurt of growth into the infinite. The paths we choose to the very end days will always provide inspiration to those looking for the deeper meaning to life and death.

All roads lead home. No matter how we get there, we will all end up with the Universal One. Paths, steep or crooked or easy, all flow from our actions and choices that lead us to the other dimension. We are all working our way through life to arrive at the One Place.

So many think their particular path is the only true way. While it may work for them, each of us is entitled to seek our own route. We all have our own unique reasons for being here and discoveries we need to make. Free will also permits us to make less than optimal choices. Then we drown in the excess of wisdomless paths. Hopefully, time will reveal to us a better route.

The grieving continues but the passage of time and keeping myself very busy with projects, including this book, have helped. For me, the clock ticks a little faster these days. I sense that the time truly is now or never to do what I most want to do. Absolutely, no one can be completely certain when that last day will dawn, so best get moving while you can. Thus, as I continue to grieve for these painful losses, I am indeed, moving on into a life that includes lots of fun and laughter and a much more purposeful bent on doing what most makes my heart sing.

Some are wise beyond their years; I believe I have become wise simply because of my years which are beginning to number too many on one end and too few at the other. Wisdom is there for all of us to find if we but look. Sometimes we stumble upon it; other times it absolutely smacks us right in the face, daring us to ignore the potential it offers.

Anything that I have offered herein still pales in comparison to all of those great communicators who have sent their wisdom out across the centuries.

Please do yourself a really great favor and release all that is negative and reach out for the good that can be received when you open to it. Please find what gives you joy. Do what makes your heart sing. Learn to dance, even if you can only do it with your fingers. Don't just sit on the sidelines while life passes you by and all you do is respond with a deep sigh. Most importantly...*love*... *love big, love deep* and show love through kindness and caring. I know I repeat myself, but love truly is all that really matters. We are all here to learn how to give and receive love. So open your hearts to the greatest gifts God offers us all. Then you will have no regrets!!!!!

And just in case you need it here is a list of many of the things I like:

- Fresh fallen snow with no tracks;
- A wooded stream rippling along;
- Mountain stillness;
- Grandchildren's hugs;
- All hugs;
- Happy babies;
- Ice cream;
- Steaming cups of tea;
- Fresh garden produce;
- Wooded walks in spring, summer, winter and fall;
- Cuddling;
- Down comforters;
- Homemade soup;
- Laughter shared with those I love;
- Good friends;
- Feelings of peace and serenity;
- Satisfaction of a job well done;

- Writing almost anything;
- Real wood fires;
- Candles, lots of candles;
- Birthdays, especially my own;
- Cooking for my grandchildren;
- Flowers, everywhere, all the time; (if I didn't know better I would think I was born in a flower, holding a candle.)
- A good hair day!

CHAPTER XI

SLICES OF LIFE

*There is an unseen life that dreams us. It knows our true
direction and destiny. We can trust ourselves more
than we realize, and we need to have no fear of change.*
John O'Donohue
Anam Cara

Journal entries begun so many years ago reveal a lot about my
thinking and the direction I was beginning to take. By reserving
this time for myself each day, I was starting to receive a glimmer
of the peace that could be found in the quiet of these moments.
As time passed, it became obvious to me that this was becoming an absolute necessity, this commune with a greater, deeper
part of me. I know for certain that my deepened connections to
Spirit and God, these strengthened bonds with entities greater
then myself, are what have aided me, carried me when I could not
walk, particularly in the midst of all that has transpired since the
beginning of 2004.

There is no life on this earth that is so serene, so perfect that it
has not been through difficulties and pain and sorrow of some
description. As I have said so often to my grandchildren, "Life is
reality in 3D Technicolor."

We live in this real world, full of love and hate, joy and horror, fulfilled lives and failed ones. Some have good health. There are others facing tremendous challenges of illness and disabilities. Too many fight for every scrap of food they eat while some dine on lobster and steak. In this great, wonderful, beautiful, free country of ours, there are lives at both ends of the spectrum and everywhere in between. But everyone is entitled to both peace and love. Those in survival mode often can't imagine such concepts. Far more, caught up in the drama of all that surrounds them, just don't have a clue that life offers them choices.

How about you? Where do you sit on the scale of love and peace, fully integrated, moving into all that can awaken in you, or so totally lost that you don't even acknowledge this place? Anything is possible and practice truly does make peace available. Even five or ten minutes of quiet for yourself each day will produce untold benefits.

There simply are not enough words for me to fully explain what I have found in my quiet moments. This daily practice of sitting in silence, along with prayer, writing and reading has continued to hold me together even when I felt I was ready to fall apart. There have been instances where I wasn't totally centered in peace but I was able to muster the courage to keep going until I could reach that place. In addition, so much has opened in my life. With more certainty than ever, I have come to resonate with what truly is the vibration of my heart's song. That is one of the greatest blessings I could ever receive for I have searched for so long. Talk about being a late bloomer. I must be one of the very last roses of summer! You know, the one that stares at you, all snow covered, totally amazed that summer has disappeared.

We all make choices and they lead us places we may never have dreamed and not always necessarily to our liking. Why? Far too often the choices are not wise ones or are born out of desperation. Life pushes us into corners sometimes and we'll take almost any way out.

After all, we have children to feed and bills to pay. Life can become littered with these moments, especially when we lack true direction.

As women, we so often get caught up in the demands of holding family and household together; trying to solve everyone else's problems. It's a great distraction and a worthy cause, but it can manage to eat up all our hours, with no time left for developing ourselves. After all, we can't be selfish, can we? A little selfish is what we all need to learn to be. We really should take some time each day and make it ours...perhaps to write, to paint, to walk, talk to ourselves; whatever it takes to find out who we really are. Maybe we want to take classes to explore a new aspect of life and broaden our horizons. I finally came to realize that it was truly essential to do whatever I needed to do to find my forgotten self.

What drives the human spirit? I think it is the will to survive and beat the odds! We can do most anything for a little while, but sometimes we end up doing it for years. We may feel caught in a trap, not believing we can do any better. We can be afraid to take a leap up the ladder. Too often we are held back simply by a lack of faith in ourselves and our abilities.

At times it can seem like there are too many roads, too many choices. Each fork can take us in a different direction. If we are not tuned into our real talents, our natural inclinations, we waste years trudging on the wrong road. Too often I knew what I didn't like, yet so seldom was I able to understand my real talents. As I have begun to follow what I perceive as my intended path, I have been able to bring a great sense of joy and satisfaction to every facet of my life.

When we are not encouraged from our young life on to explore the world and see what best fits, then we should do it as soon as we can as adults. It will take courage to explore and see what avenues we can open to lead to a more satisfying life. Start by joining groups, taking classes, volunteering, and talking to others about their interests. Spend some time enjoying new activities or ones that you felt interested in as a child. You will soon be able to sort out what best fits your life now and brings you enjoyment.

Now more than ever, I strive for increased enlightenment, continue to ask for direction and work at what I now feel is my true calling. I want to put the time I have left into writing and helping others discover their own peace.

Until recently I was still not sure I could accomplish anything of note in terms of writing, having for years questioned my abilities. Years ago I penned:

I can't believe I can do this and wonder if it will appear to be too trite. I am still not sure what inner well it all flows from. It now delights me to have this flow and why I would question the source is unclear. Why do I care? I don't have to explain my muse to anyone. I am just grateful that it exists and is now coming forth. I believe it has been buried for too long. Maybe it just took this long for the seeds to germinate.

To encourage you on your own way I have included bits and pieces of my own journey. These are thoughts, ideas, concepts that I jotted down as they came to me. They may not be the most profound or awe inspiring. It is possible that what will help you the most is to simply see it truly is in the ordinary that you can find the extraordinary if you are willing to look. May you find something here that will light a spark inside you and send you off to pursue whatever it takes to make your heart sing.

I continue to journal thoughts, feelings, messages, and poems daily...whatever comes out the end of my pen. What follows is just a small portion of the last 20 years. Most of the entries have come from the latest years because they detail my greatest struggles

The §§ separates journal entries.

§§

2002

Spring is here and this is my 66ᵗʰ year and things are a' changing. Good, I need more positives in my life. I cannot allow myself to worry about what I cannot control. It wastes my time and energy and solves nothing. Kiss it up to God and be done with it. That is all there is. It does not pay to get too attached to any of these possessions for they can all too quickly disappear. They are of no use when we pass and just stay behind for someone else to sort through.

I must trust that God will take care of everything. In His infinite wisdom He has all the important answers and solutions.

§§

*How truly wonderful a gift it is to find at least one person who, in deed and action, simply allows you to be. No matter your age or stage, you can move on to more important things. Sometimes self-acceptance arrives with growing older and coming to understand that you **always** were okay. It is never too late.*

§§

I cannot question what lessons belong to others. I have enough struggle and learning with my own. The answers all lie within but it can take a lifetime to uncover them, yet it is well worth the

*effort. It does take work. You cannot live the shallow life and fig-
ure out what it's all about.*

*Truly the most important thing is love. Love yourself because
if you don't, who will besides God and He always loves you
no matter what! Love others, because, just like you, everyone
needs the warmth and encouragement that love provides. I
realize I need to practice every day being more aware of others, seeing if I can help them move more smoothly through life.*

§§

2003

*Maybe I was meant to be a hermit, a recluse. But then, how would
I ever laugh alone? Life is such a trade-off.*

§§

*The flow of the days seems to almost spin out of control it goes so
quickly. It rounds the corner of the mornings, melting them into
afternoons. The pace quickens when darkness seeps in and then
it starts all over again.*

§§

2005

*Sometimes I have to consciously turn that deep internal button
from unworthiness to fully worthy...knowing that this grace has
been there all along. Realizing once again, that I only manifest
what I truly feel, I have to return myself again and again, when I*

get too far off key. Only if I make this choice that is best for me and stay aware of where I truly need to be can I hold onto this place until the effort becomes a stream and the passion of peace flows like a calm river through every facet of the jewel that is my life.

§§

2006

In the stillness of the morning I open my heart to all that is positively possible. May my day be healthy and whole and joyful. Let me take time to listen to the birds' songs, a child's question, the softness of the new day. Let me carry God's love all through these hours as I work and play.

I wrap these moments around me, hoping to carry them with me. Sometimes I win, sometimes I lose when I get wrapped up in the drama around me. The most I can do for others these days is to offer an ear, moral support, and if possible, a helping hand.

§§

We all need unconditional love so that we know that we are accepted for who we are and that who we are is really okay. Knowing or learning we are okay helps us move forward a little faster. Otherwise we use up too much energy fighting to maintain our balance and hold onto our place in the world.

We don't need to pay so much attention if any, to those on the fringes but it is the ones closest to us who are bound to have the greatest affect. If they can't accept us and keep trying to mold us into their desired image, then who are we? We can become a hermit to lessen the pressure, but we absolutely need some love and companionship from others. Some can rise above the criticism and move on while others stay stuck.

§§

Be still and calm the mind's chatter. Listen to the birds' songs who sing because they can. What would you do simply for the joy of doing, knowing that you could? Knowing that God has given you this ability but you are too fearful of: 1) failure; 2) what others think; 3) because you've always been told that you couldn't because you are too ugly, dumb, fat/thin, old/young, rich/poor, whatever!? Learn to ignore all this and let your heart awaken to a greater sense of who you really are and what your real gifts and talents hold for you. Figure out how to allow yourself to delight in the joys that make your toes curl! Yes, get into the groove of opening to that song long buried in your heart.

§§

There is no way to change all that has happened in these past weeks and there is still much that needs finalized. But it will get done and life will continue, albeit, changed in immeasurable ways. Such is the fabric of life, sometimes smooth as silk, sometimes tougher than rawhide; too often torn and mended into a different weave. Still, it goes on yard after yard, year after year. So I must continue to move forward, for I have much yet to accomplish and people depending on me. And so it is.

§§

The days tumble down a black endless hole like snowflakes in an avalanche, driven by the sheer force of doing.

§§

Are we building monuments to the future or memorials to the past? What meaning is there to this endless parade of paper shuffling? Like a fly stuck on an endless treadmill, we're going nowhere. This merry-go-round never stops and the music grinds on, a tinny tune.

§§

I am so thankful to be in this moment. I feel so much joy, especially when I sit here and just give myself to this time of quiet, of so much peace. Indeed, I am blessed to have such an abundance of abilities and they really are beginning to blossom. I am so very, very lucky to have, at last, come into this place in my life. So many things have had to happen to bring me here. It is amazing how it falls into place when so often the paths have been murky and cluttered with the debris of choices that sent me in circles to learn the lessons needed before I could reach this beautiful place. Have I arrived at my destiny? Hardly! This is just another stepping stone on the journey for the questing is indeed what it is all about. In truth, the journey is never over for any who seek the knowingness that leads to Spirit. I am so blessed.

(At that time I did not realize just how sorely I would soon be tested. The preceding was written about five weeks before my older son died.)

§§

What does it all mean, anyway? Find it difficult to always keep pushing when nothing feels like it works. Of course, how do I know if it works? I just swim around and around in a very small pond! I'd get out and move to a fresh one if I could figure out how. But then, I would have to leave everything behind, so that's not a good plan. Besides, I can't shed what is inside, for the pain would travel with me. Nothing can be accomplished by running away. I seem to be tired of taking care of others. If something happened to me the world would collectively shrug its shoulders and move on. Then, again, there is only so much other people can do. I have to do the hard parts myself. Gee, right now I don't much like that idea and am not sure how to continue. Of course, I want it all over as of yesterday. I want my life back the way it was. I realize there are valuable lessons here and in time I will absorb them and move on. Right now I'm kicking and screaming in protest! Everything feels so meaningless.

§§

Life truly becomes jam packed with things...things that must be done. Too much crams our lives full and complicates everything. Yet, people are eager for more things all the time. The stores are busy with those who seek to fill the hole inside. There is nothing they can buy that will do the job. Truly do I know there is not one single thing out there anywhere that will replace the loss of my son.

§§

Too much, too much, too much! Feel as if I would like to open up the top of my head, dump all this stuff out and start over fresh.

§§

If all we get is rain, do we make mud pies or just wallow in the puddles, digging the hole deeper and deeper?

§§

So much of our attention, time and energy is focused on the attainment of something down the road we view as better than where we are now. Yet, when that thing or moment arrives, the experience can be far less than what we hoped for. Would it not be much more enriching to take the dailyness we allow to pass largely unnoticed beneath our feet, and embrace it in the moment? Why not enjoy and immerse ourselves in the love and goodness that is being offered right now? None of us know when the final curtain will fall and there is no more.

§§

It is always, always difficult to be patient. Because I kept wanting to move into that "something better" place too much has been missed in the moment because it never seemed good enough. Before I knew it, 70 years had passed and I still didn't feel I had fully arrived at my "something better". It all seems like a carrot just ahead of the leading horse in a race, never attainable.

Now I finally realize that only I can work on my inner self so I can move forward on my journey. Everything in my life is what I have already invited in. All my past actions, thoughts and relationships have carried over to right now. What I have is exactly what I have asked for, whether or not I want to admit it. If I **really** *desire something different, I need to understand on a deeper level that I need to change in order to create the desired shift. I'm the only one who can get myself going in the direction that God wishes I would choose. I must find my own resources, of which there are plenty. Once I truly open to this path, all I need will be made available.*

§§

Perhaps I need to express more deep gratitude for what I do have and for all my awakening thus far. It may be that in the very ordinariness of my everyday life lies my greatest opportunity to do the most good. It is so easy to become lost in the chaos of lives submerged in all manner of churning energies. It is nice to feel calm and centered, even if only for this short time, but it does set the tone for my day.

§§

2007

Peace wraps itself around me like a mantle. It is still just now, for not even the birds seem to be singing. Some mornings seem to be such noisy affairs. This is truly the easiest thing I do each morning. I never seem to lack for words flowing from the end of my pen. It is such a pleasure to write each day. Why I ever got away from it I don't know.

§§

Difficult to know what to do and where I am headed when I fail to seek out the wisdom and advice that I know is available to me. Why is this? Do I delight, somehow, in the turmoil and sadness of my current "story"? Habits, long ago formed, run deep. I do believe there must be some time permitted for myself to grieve and so much was so chaotic from the start. So how do I temper things to my satisfaction never mind anyone else's? How do I live with the never answered questions and are they all that important anyway? I did to the best of my ability at any given time in the life of my son and did what I could to help; surely that had to demonstrate love. The ways that I was amiss with him are no longer correctable. It is done; it is finished and all is well everywhere.

Perhaps, in grief, the biggest part is our own feeling of having somehow failed the one who is no longer physically among us. Do we always feel we have fallen short in ways that only we notice? If so, the lessons may be to do as much as possible for those still around us. Then we should perhaps top it with a healthy dose of self-forgiveness. In the long run, even these efforts may not satisfy us, but we have much to learn.

§§

2008

Take your lessons from the earth which will turn green again and renew itself once more. Every day we have a new opportunity to turn our lives around, learn from the past and move on in love and peace and help others to do the same. Remember to be thankful for the past and the present. They both provide us with opportunity and help mold us into who we are.

§§

Trying to hold on to a tiny bit of peace and quiet for just a little while. So much to do and I am tired of doing, but life marches on and it is best to stay in the flow. What do I really want? The answer is peace and quiet, time to contemplate, and freedom from so much doing for these few minutes so I can figure out where I am. A little pampering would be nice! More rest, less stress, more trust, less worry.

§§

No doubt one of my greatest concerns has become running out of time on this planet. It seems that I'll never get wherever it is I think I should have advanced to but that may simply be the nature of the whole routine. No need to panic; just keep working in my desired direction and be open to whatever insight I can gain. I must learn to appreciate more what time I have left with my husband and look for the lessons in the relationship as well as with all things. Try harder to be nicer and more loving and forgiving with all those I come in contact with. That is really all the Universe asks for anyway.

§§

It would be so wonderful to go to sleep and wake up, clear about what to do and how to do it and no worries about the time and money it takes.

§§

Yesterday when I sat here and looked out at the heart shaped space in the spruce branches, I thought of my dad and the love between us. As I realized that this love was really the only important thing, then all the pain, anger, feeling cheated, etc., about his estate just fell away. Now I know I am ready to move on.

§§

2009

We don't get second changes on so many things so why is it so hard to do it right the first time? Life can become so full of regrets: can't undo, re-do, change so many things. The important thing must be...do we learn from any of it? Can we find the lesson that the moment holds? We have to move on, regardless.

§§

I am trying harder to just go with the flow and live more in the present. I have come to realize how very focused I have been for a long time on some distant future. Somehow I seem to regard where I am and have been, for the past few years, as a temporary situation. If things would only move aside, I could get on with a better life. Most definitely I need to continue to work on the here and now, letting it flow and accepting that this is my life. This means meeting the challenges and integrating all my knowledge so I can turn it into wisdom and help others understand the lessons that are to be learned.

§§

The birds' songs and the soft, warm air grace these moments of my quiet meditation, so peaceful, so serene, so necessary to the start of my day. Later, summer will lace its heat through the afternoon hours, providing the warmth to make my garden grow. For now it is delightfully just right for sitting here and drawing the peace around me. This special place and these tranquil moments help me to begin my day in love and patience. They are as cherished as anything in my life could possibly be. The hours of duty will soon call and I will then move forward into this new day, knowing I can return again and again to be refreshed once more.

§§

What am I doing in this moment? Nothing!? It can't be nothing because I am still breathing and thinking. The oxygen fuels the brain. Only without the breath would there be nothing, at least here. Who knows what is on the other side?

So, as I breathe, I think but do I monitor my thoughts or just let them run wild? Just now it seems to be half and half... some random, some held in check. I should be more careful and treat my thoughts like gold nuggets. They will determine the direction of my day and my interactions with others. That is the reason I seek out the quiet space in the early morning...to set the tone for all that follows.

§§

July slides away like a log on a downhill skid, taking the lushness of summer with it. Too quickly it will become August and, whoosh! The summer has disappeared replaced by the delights of September. That pregnant month...September... with all of its richness and ripeness, bursting with blossom and fruit; heavy laden, it waddles into October for the annual harvest of earth's bounty.

§§

2010

Hurry is not my best word so early in the morning anymore. I want softness, peace, quiet, the song of the birds. I want time to think, to muse, to pray and write. I like to gather all this around me like a cloak and bask in the warmth and the comfort all this offers me. This is the part of the day that helps me stay centered in the other hours. This is truly my refuge and my strength that radiates from knowing that all is always well. It is here that I open myself to the possibilities that life and each day has to offer. I still need to slow down some so that I don't miss out on what is being opened to me. Also, I need to be more alert to the energies around me. Everything unfolds in its own time...even me!

§§

When I miss out on something the Universe offers me does it bring it back around or is it gone forever? The answer I get is, "Yes, sometimes, other times it's a once in a lifetime, but you haven't missed much!"

§§

Each road I have taken has found me in places I couldn't have imagined. But, in the end they have all led me here, where I am today. That is all I need to know. I cannot go back now and choose other paths that would send me in a different direction. I can only watch now for new opportunities and try to make better decisions with mindfulness. I do not know how much future my life holds. Like everyone, I only have today. May I use it as the gift that it is.

§§

How I wish I could feel that every day is filled to the brim with exceptional accomplishment. Alas, life is so ordinary and filled with more drudge than song. Could it be that I don't appreciate what I do accomplish because it is not difficult? Why do I not give myself credit for what good I do, especially when these things are done from the love in my heart?

§§

I have taken too much to heart words spoken by others that do not ring true to my ears. Why do I allow them to color my mood and future? Can I not decide these things for myself? Where is my inner voice and why am I not listening to it? My mind seems filled with the fog I see outside my window.

§§

I know that, inside me there is a calm space and I need to go there every day. How else can I weather the bumps and lumps that fall onto my life's plate? A plate that too often of late, seems overflowing with tasks and toils and others' needs. How else can I muster the strength and courage to go on? Yet, I know I will go on, because I always have, because I survive, no matter what, thanks to all the help the Universe, my spirit guides and archangels provide. As always, it is a journey cushioned by all the help and comfort and peace that floods my being.

§§

Listening to the sounds of the water fountain I imagine myself dissolving like melted ice into the water's flow; no longer distinguishable from any other single drop, simply part of the whole. I am flowing along without resistance in this stream, allowing the peace of the Universe's plan to move me along. Wanting for nothing; after all, what does water need? I wish to flow through rain, sun and snow to become one with the great ocean of Life.

§§

Be peace...wherever and everywhere you are. Be that calm in the middle of all storms. Show the world and all around you that peace is possible. Breathe peace; cultivate peace as you would your plants; make peace your garden. Encourage it to grow and spread until you are completely surrounded by peace and it is all you can feel. Know that as you grow in peace, this peace will grow in you. Breathe peace in and out until that is all you are.

§§

Being my impatient Aries self, I sometimes wish life was a giant chalkboard and I could just erase all the parts I would like to do without. Yet, I realize that the less desirable parts of my life knit together with the more welcome ones to make up this person that I am. To learn our truths we have to work through the ugly along with the more lovely aspects that appear on our path. Only then can we be whole as opposed to seeing ourselves in little bits and pieces, scattered across our years. It is also important to realize that the task is never complete. I, like everyone else, will always be a work of art in the making, untitled and forever unfinished.

2011

The wind blows and the chimes sing their song as the thunder rolls across the sky. The birds keep searching for their morsels. The world stops neither for rain nor wind nor death nor destruction. It continues to be. We continue to breathe. No matter how great the tragedy...large and small ones circle us every day...existence continues.

The world stops not for your pain or mine. It simply absorbs it into its bosom and continues to breathe. So, too, we must find the courage and the will to go on...just breathe, one breath at a time.

§§

There are so many firsts in life; first breath, first tooth, first step, first love and on the list goes. We anticipate and generally welcome these firsts as milestones along the road of life. Some of the lasts are just as welcome; last mortgage or car payment, last exam of a difficult course, last child graduates. But the timetable is hidden from us on so many finals; last hug, last kiss, last words from a loved one. Even if we realize the end is near we cannot be certain when it will arrive. We do not even know when our own last breath will be counted. We can only do what needs done and spread joy and love throughout what days we have.

§§

Who stole my summer away when I wasn't looking; robbing me of the warm sunshine, bright skies and cheerful flowers? Wasn't I paying enough attention? Surely it wasn't because summer is too short here! No! Never! It must be that I, in some way failed to fully appreciate all the glory laid out before me. So now it is being taken away, one bloom, one leaf at a time. There is no way to bring it back. Upon its return it will never be quite the same. I must learn to inhale more deeply of each day, for the years pass too swiftly, taking those we hold dear, leaving empty places in our hearts.

Friendships, like flowers, bloom and sometimes fade, especially if we don't tend them enough. It also may just be that their time is done. Like summer, the days are numbered for all that lives.

Take more time to enjoy what is before you right now. Always remember, nothing is so terrible that you won't come out the other side.

§§

And so it goes...life contains so many surprises and we cannot always anticipate their arrival or content. We just have to keep moving and work at going in the directions that our gut indicates and believe in ourselves and our right to be where we are.

I, myself, have gone in so many directions that in retrospect, now seem so wrong, so far afield. The important point is that I eventually got to where I am now. Who is to say I was wrong; I wasn't listening, etc.? It is all a learning experience I truly know. The most important thing is to learn to listen to the gut as it will never fail you. We have a fail proof radar system that we greatly underutilize. It contains all the wisdom we will ever need.

§§

My life has been blessed by all who have entered it, some on a positive vibration, others less so. All learning is a blessing and has served to put me right where I am today. I thank all creation for where I am. I am proud of myself.

§§

My thoughts are like crashing waves upon the shore of my mind, slipping back out to the great ocean of nothingness before I can grasp them. Churning and turning, am I never at rest? Where is the calm I have known in the past? How do I recapture what has held me steadfast? All this debris finds the crack in the door of my mind, sticks a foot in and then sidles in to run amok through the moment, tumbling over and spilling back out.

§§

In the realm of the goodness of life resides my morning time filled with stillness that becomes enhanced by the songs of the birds. We are at peace, these birds and I, doing our daily morning thing. Each in perfect alignment with the greater whole that is equal to the sum of its parts that includes us. We reside here in love and perfection, because we are right where we are supposed to be. The Universe has all the answers. We are the ones who forget to ask the right questions. So be still and listen, for it all lies within, just waiting for us to turn the key that opens the door of inner knowing.

I know I possess the courage to open new doors for myself and continue to discover the delights, the peace, the love the Universe always holds for me. I said years ago, after a fire took our home and possessions, the world stops for nothing, no matter how great or small the tragedy. It keeps turning and as long as I breathe I must be willing to continue to live as fully as possible.

§§

Despite the losses, life goes on for me and I certainly am in no hurry to depart. I do have things I want to do and I just want to enjoy living and learning and sharing my understanding of what I believe we are here for. I really like getting others to stop and think about more than the surface stuff.

§§

2012

These days, the only age that looks really old to me is maybe 100. Where did all these years go; how did they slip by so quickly? And they seem to be going faster all the time! Who reset the clock to fast and faster? I always tell anyone younger when they moan about how old they are, that I will happily trade my years for theirs! But, in truth would I? Who wants to do all that again unless I can change a few things? Besides, if I could make changes I wouldn't come out of the experiences quite the same. At this point I really am satisfied with where I am and who I have become. I believe that the past has provided what I needed to make my way here.

§§

Why has it taken all these years to finally find my most purposeful way? Or is it just that all this time, all these experiences, the love, the loss, the pain were required, much like good seasoning and aging, for me to become this Ageless Sage? Could it be that I am simply my own Ageless Sage and no one else's? Or am I both? Is it too soon to tell, or maybe too late to matter? What's the difference? There always have been questions and there always will be. All that went on before us and continues beyond us will result in questions. If it were not so, no one would ever seek the answers that awaken them to a fuller life.

Is it even possible to answer such a question to one's satisfaction, as everyone you ask would voice their own opinion. Perhaps, in truth, the answer only really matters to me, thus I should only ask the question of myself.

§§

Someday, maybe, I'm going to sit down with all my little scraps of paper and call all these unidentifiable phone numbers just to see who is at the other end. Hopefully, it will remind me why I wrote the dang thing down in the first place.

§§

Certainly if you don't ever try anything outside of your per-ceived safety zone, you take no risks and you never fail. But, oh, what a narrow life you live! Is there not one shred of adventure nestled deep in your soul? Do you not long to be free; to taste just a little more of what the world and life have to offer? Where is the song that will really make your heart sing? How is it that I have dared to try so much? I did find I wasn't equally talented at everything I chose to experience. Marriage might be considered one of my less stellar successes. However I did keep trying until I got that right!

§§

A lot of success in doing something is simply the fun, the enjoyment you experience when you are doing it. No need to win acclaim or external reward. The real reward comes from knowing you tried, had a good time and either found a new interest or are open to moving on to something else.

§§

Why am I always so anxious to move forward? What is it I seek that I cannot find here and now? If I do not put more physical effort into making changes on a day-to-day basis why do I expect tomorrow, next month, next year will be that much different?

§§

I have reached a point in my life, finally, where I want to control where I am going and what I am doing. A trade off, yes, because I leave a lot behind but the dust doesn't catch in my throat anymore. So I'm off and running toward goals that I never before dreamed could become reality. Sometimes I can even slow to a walk or a crawl. Then I stop to enjoy the sunshine on a warm spring day and hours spent with my grandchildren that they and I will always cherish. I now do what I do because it is what I choose.

§§

What is life? A collection of years, deeds, relationships, lessons learned, forgotten and relearned. Love and be loved, helping others, helping our-selves; all of this and more. Sometimes little of it, by itself, makes any sense. The only foundation that keeps one on any kind of an even keel is to find God in all of it. And to keep on loving and doing, no matter what we are faced with. Love others and love ourselves and know each life matters to Him. Else all is for naught. These thoughts barely scratch the surface of what is.

§§

Why is everyone in such an unconscious state, such a rush all the time? Slow down. You'll still get where you are going and be calmer as well.

§§

The small things in life can bring much delight if we just notice them and pay closer attention. Too often we scurry by, oblivious to all of God's handiwork that surrounds us. Better to enjoy enjoy a scarlet cardinal perched on the evergreen bough; the bright yellow daffodil daring to open to the sunny but chilly spring day; the aroma of good food; the overabundance of bright produce at the market; a baby's cooing; a child's sweet smile as you pass.

§§

How about, just for one day, we all slow our steps and smile at everyone we encounter. You will be surprised at how much better you feel.

§§

What is life but a brief moment upon this Shakespearian stage, a few dramas and we return to our true space. If we could but realize how quickly this time will pass and how much needs done for others, perhaps more would make better use of this existence called life.

§§

What am I trying to accomplish in my life? What is beneath this drive to do, be more, better, greater? Do I feel something is missing? Am I somehow lacking, inadequate? Why do I feel guilty if I think I'm not doing a big enough job?

Why is laughter so rewarding? I just know it feels good. The after effects of laughter are long lasting and can be pulled from the memory at will to be relished over and over again. In that, I truly am my father's daughter, for he loved to laugh, as well.

§§

No matter who you are, life is never one big flashy experience after another. No one could sustain it. I have come to realize that the truly meaningful times in our lives occur in small doses. They involve those we love and often the lasting value is not totally appreciated until later. We are just doing what we do...living. Now, as I look back on the expanse of a long life I see these bits and pieces for what they are, a life lived with humor and, I'd like to think, grace. A life filled with mistakes balanced by learning and the ability to move on. Strength that has come through my genes and sustained me that I can see is being passed down through my grand-children.

It truly is the small things that matter most; a kind word, a smile, laughter shared. They all add up until they blossom into a life well lived, but it's a secret that doesn't reveal itself until near the end.

§§

The peace that comes to me as I sit here even on a Monday morning is priceless. Despite all that has taken place, my life is good. I find so much joy in my morning solitude, my gardens, my flowers, my music, my musings, my friends. What more could I ask for? A barrel of $20s, as my friend Ellare likes to say.

§§

In all the layers of life there is so much to explore, to share with others, to nudge open minds and hearts. Life can be so interesting and I pray I find it so, just as Milo did.

§§

Regardless of what I have felt in the past as to whether or not I was loved and loving toward others, a new day has opened to reveal how much love is coming to me. I have to be a willing receptacle, gently allowing myself to receive what others are willing to give. We are all loved by the Great One Universal God and there are no strings attached. He would like us to share this love with everyone. But His love can seem more difficult to identify with because we sense almost everything on a physical level. We are accustomed to love coming to us on the basis of hugs and verbal clues.

This newly acquired opening to love has not come easily to me who always felt somehow deficient. For so long it seemed I just couldn't quite find the element of living that would make me feel acceptable and therefore, loved. But that is all in the past. I have grown to truly like myself and my presence in the world. Age does have advantages not afforded to the young. Still, it should not take a lifetime to realize that one is okay. **We are all okay every day.** *Opening to the love that flows to me, particularly from those in spirit is one of the few things that is providing me with a deep, inner peace. Life is irrevocably changed for me and this is leading to new pathways both in my heart and in my interaction with the world around me. One goal is to be kinder, more caring and less judgmental to all whose lives I touch in any way.*

§§

I am sick of so much stuff weighing me down. I really would like things much simpler and far less cluttered, cleared out and cleaned up. How long will it take me to get there? It seems like the rest of my life. Just have to keep working at all of it, but I don't have as much push as I once did.

§§

I am content to be where I am right now. The sadness will pass and I will be right where I need to be. Life goes on and I can choose to flow with it in my own little stream or sit in a corner and let it pass me by. Since I was never good at corners, I'm not sitting. Just because my front porch is filled with rocking chairs doesn't mean I am stuck there. I am rocking for sure as

I continue to drum, sing, garden, and write. Life keeps moving and I intend to stay in the flow. I promise myself I will get through this.

§§

Life is a journey with a destination that so many dread... death. No one I presently know is eager to reach that final breath. So why do we rush through life so fast? How much better it would be to extract the honey from every moment and cherish the love that is such a gift to us all, whether we give or receive.

Surround yourself with all the love that comes to you from those around you as well as the love that comes from the other side. In turn, send out love to everyone you have any contact with. Small acts of kindness, gentle words and hugs and smiles can spread a lot of love. Be the light that erases the darkness. Be the seed of joy that can blossom anywhere and everywhere. Be the mirror to inspire and enlighten others so they can reflect in it and spread that reflection into their circle of love.

§§

The rest of my life looms large just now. I realize my days are dwindling down, even if I might have 20 years left. How can I make each day count? I must do my best and try to help others even as I help myself. My goal is to introduce fun, joy, insight to everyone I can reach. All I can do is introduce the concepts. On their own they will pick up or drop the ball as they experience the doors that open in their own way, their own time.

§§

I am in love with the quiet early morning moments that I seek. Herein resides all the gifts God brings to me, to be shared and echoed throughout my day.

§§

We are all seeking the same thing...reunion with the highest part of ourselves on the soul level. How much can we transform while we are still here?

§§

Have to wonder why we only find beauty in sunny days as opposed to cloudy ones which we declare as being ugly. Rather like many other things in life, we are so superficial and all too often only see the obvious so we don't have to look beneath what stares us in the face. The path of least resistance fails us because we then miss out on a lot of more important things.

There actually is a great deal more in my journals I wrote as I wound through the days. However, I feel I have included enough, if not maybe too much to chart my course along this path of loss, grief and continuing recovery that nobody is anxious to walk. I believe what I have written demonstrates how these experiences have reshaped me into a stronger, more focused on the positive, person that I have become.

I now realize it shows that we all have the strength to overcome even the most profound losses and continue to find some joy in life. It just takes time and making the choice to keep on experiencing life.

CHAPTER XII

MY INNER VOICE

If, in your travels, you can't find God, you have not journeyed deep enough into your own heart and soul.
Bob Luckin
Science of Mind

As I became more faithful with my journal writing, a little voice inside me somewhere began to send messages out through the end of my pen. I was instructed to be faithful to the task and not stop my daily practice. However, twice I returned to the workforce and so temporarily ended my usual writing. I wrote when I could but the messages only returned when I was meditating and writing faithfully again every day. I have not received any for a long time.

There is no easy way to explain how they came to me. Suffice to say that, once I sat down with pen in hand and an open journal, the words simply spilled out onto the page. I apologize for none of it.

My life has been so filled with ups and downs that my writing efforts can often be overlooked. The messages didn't flow when I was not faithful to the task. It may have been because I allowed myself to get too involved in the world in the mornings rather than rise and go straight to my quiet space.

Surely we are all entitled to be open and aware of our own inner guidance and whispers from the Universe that surround us daily. The most important aspects are to be present and to learn to pay attention and ask to be shown. Everyone has this ability if they are interested in developing it. Included here are a few of these messages.

§§

Peace be with you and all around you. You have all the strength you need to go on, regardless of what life dishes up. You are well anchored and secure. Learn to smile more...it will open doors. Take life as it comes; there is naught you can do otherwise. Learn to live more simply. It is easier and does not cost as much. No one needs all this stuff that people fill their lives with. If they have Me they lack for nothing. Be still, I am always here. People forget Me until they need Me; then they don't know where to find Me. I am always here and I am always everywhere...in the air that you breathe, in the plants and flowers and trees. I abide deep inside you. Be still, I say, be still. I am always with you. Look to Me daily and you will never be in want. Your mind wanders, try to keep it here.

§§

Stick with those that love you unquestionably and be reluctant to open the door of friendship until you truly know who knocks there. Be alert. Light yourself with the light that keeps you safe and thus draws like-minded souls to you. Don't be flashy or arrogant or ever think you know it all. One lifetime is never enough to complete this education. You will come back. There are many lessons to learn. You are still to heal but you don't have all the knowledge. You have done well and made much progress, but you still have farther to go. I will lead the way. You must, however, be open and alert to the doors I offer you. I am with you, always. Deep inside you is a well that is yet untapped. Soon the information it contains will flow through you. I will show you how to use it. It is yours but it comes from Me. Be grateful I have chosen you to share this with the others. You seem reluctant to believe what I am telling you here. Yes, I read your mind! Understand that you are the vessel I have chosen to fill. You are the messenger who will become the message. No matter what comes to you, what troubles, I will allow nothing to harm you. Do not listen to the others. You are mine. Go in peace and serve the Lord.

§§

Let peace fill you to the bone and beyond. Breathe in deep so that the peace holds to carry you through your day. Let the peace flow through you and out into all you meet that they may understand by seeing what real peace means. Peace can strengthen the soul and soften a harsh attitude. It can spread caring and love to all you touch.

§§

Write, I keep saying. Write on a daily basis and much wisdom will come to your words and you will help others.

§§

Wisdom...you have a wisdom, an inner knowing and you can help others. Write and it will come to you.

§§

Let there be light; new light that shines only love unto all who people the world. My word is still good. Renew your faith. Be cheerful to all. Your needs are being taken care of. Trust; trust that I know more than you. I will not put you in harm's way. Look within rather than without, for guidance. Your guides will not fail you. Be at peace; there are more wonders than you know. Be good, be kind. Others hurt too. Listen. You will be surprised at what you hear. Tune your ears to hear that which comes from within. It is more precious than all the richest noise without. I am not finished yet! You are not too old; you have much wisdom to share. I will help you. Know that I love you. Go forth; energy will empower you. Listen each morning for my words. You're in too big a hurry to listen to more.

§§

Go forth in the world; tell them the truth. Let go and let God. Find yourself a _____?? (last word was not clear). From this place of confusion I shall become clear. Soon there will be time. Life is short; you will see. You stand to lose many you love...life will go on. Be of good cheer; I will lead you. No one can take Me away from you. I am always here for you. You are okay in My book. Be open to guidance and love; it comes in many forms. Look for it under little rocks more than in the great mountains. It comes in very ordinary forms. Be not given to great good works, but go with the everyday good and simple things you can do for others. Be kind to yourself. I will not judge you as harshly as you judge yourself. I am far kinder than others would have you believe. Why have I chosen you? Because you will do this well (keep going, there is more to come). Let your light burn brightly in this world of sadness and pain; others need your healing. I am preparing you now; you will soon see.

Go forth, with joy in your heart, for you I have chosen. I am the Alpha and Omega and you are My child. My message is simple: L O V E, love Me, love yourself, love others, love all. Go forth in joy and gladness. Love them all as children of God. They are all Mine and I love them all; can you do less? Know that all will open before you; be not afraid. You are okay and you are doing what you need to do, taking care of Milo. He loves you; be warm in his love and remember it always. No, this is not your imagination, this is really from Me. I will talk to you as much as you want to hear Me. Come to Me every day; together we will accomplish much. You are free to go.

§§

Go to that place of greater light within you. That is the place from which you must write.

§§

Peace, be at peace, for all is well and you will survive all that comes as you have already done. Keep working with Kathy for she is of much help. Keep your appointments with God each day for it is truly something you need to do and it does help you center. You need to write more. Try to get better organized to have more time for the important things; let some of the others go. Just relax; you are doing okay and making progress. You are too "tight." You should by now be able to do this without stopping to dot the i's, etc. Be still, be still; come back into the cocoon of stillness and

*warmth where you find Me. Forgive yourself for what you con-
sider your shortcomings. You do well with things (life). Allow
yourself more time to grieve. You have not been able to do so, but
have just pushed it aside. You need to do this before the next loss
hits. Yet, look forward and know it is all okay; it will all work out.
Take time to think things through...do not rush to judgment or
decisions or anything. Yes, you will get your class work done and
done well. You will have to decide how you want to use it, where
you want to help, how you can help. It is up to you but you will
be able to help many. Do not judge these words you receive; just
write them down. You need to spend more time here with Me. I
will see that you get up earlier so that you can. Thank you.*

§§

*Be more open...be more still...be here. Do not be afraid and we
don't think you are. Stillness is good for you. The quiet holds you.
Just try to be open to what we have to tell you. It will come to
you, impatient Aries! You still have trouble understanding us but
this writing is working well. We will reveal more and more to
you, just keep working with us. Your life will change in unex-
pected ways. You have much to offer others and will be able to
help them move through life events easier. Go with your gut. You
still have to do all the ordinary life things while on the earth. That
is as it should be. We are with you always. You must learn to ask
us for more. We are willing to help you. You are a child of God,
a child of the Universe. You have much to accomplish before you
go, but you also have more learning to do before you can move
on to do other things. You are soon coming in to your own. Life
will change and you will grieve but you will go on. Your time will
not come for a while, years, so do not worry over it. We love you
and will help you; just ask.*

§§

You love your children and grandchildren and would like to do more to help them. You will, and soon. Be at peace with where they are. They have much to learn and you cannot do it for them. You will do what you can. Trust that all is well for them as it is for you. You are where you need to be in their lives for now. These are waiting days. Just do what you do and do it well. It all counts. Their guardian angels are with them and they need to learn to ask for help. You can teach them, for they respect you.

§§

You need to take more time; you need more silence, more quiet in order to get it together. Too much hurry, too much push is surrounding your days, too many people to please. You need to be more independent of all these demands and you soon will be. Just be patient, your time will soon be coming to accomplish more and to have greater abundance. You need to learn to have a sharper focus as your efforts become greatly scattered now. There are so many who need your love; it is well that you help them. Be at peace with where you are just now. Keep working at this and other projects to increase your knowledge. It is good you are learning to call on us more and it is good that you do so. We will help you always. Seek our guidance more and more, and we will show you what you need to be doing. We want you to help others and you will come into your own way in that, soon. We know you intend to do good. You will also talk with others, alone and in small groups, in order to help them find their way to abundant living. We hold you in the light.

You know what to do and for the most part, you are doing it. It is important to process your grief. Yet, do not blame yourself for what was not. The past is non-existent. You only have today to make things count. Don't worry about your heart. You will be okay for the time to come. You have much work to do and you must focus on it. You must also take care of the loved one with you. His time is not that much longer. Remember to do it in joy and love. You are willing, but your sadness has taken hold. Do not sit in it too long, else it will change your whole path and that is not desirable.

Your current path is right and true for you. You have simply stopped briefly to rest before moving on. Work daily to maintain balance and restore yourself to your work. Sometimes you will make rapid progress and at times, things will slow down so you can better absorb that which you are learning. Remember all is love and all is as it should be. There are no "earth" answers for some things and this is one of them. Your work has not finished, it is only just begun. Do not be impatient with those who do not understand for they mean well. We love you and will help you always. We are always here for you. And so it is.

You must learn to be free in your heart and mind. Nothing else matters. Understand there are things you must do that you don't always understand the underlying reasons. You can see the obvious, surface reasons. Nothing lasts forever, and this having to work will not be for much longer. A year will see you in a different place. Hang tough; you will move on. Keep your focus on where you want it to be. It will happen. You know that things can change in the blink of an eye and they will. You have your inner freedom and you can manifest more outer freedom. You are working on that and we are with you all the way. Do not lose sight of your goals. You are meant to do the good that you desire. Your complete freedom will soon come.

§§

You are right. You need to be outside more. Just being able to sit in quiet amidst it all is good for you. You never seem to get out doors much and you do need to do that. You need the connection; you could have visitors if you try it. The woods still belong to you but you are reluctant to try the hill; lazy or fear of hip pain?

This message was sent to me through someone else:

We hear you. We are answering. This is the truth of the matter. There are many guiding forces at play in your life that includes your role in others' lives. You have wished it so. There is no easy or hard, for this is all agreed upon and therefore just as it should be. But, the body is absorbing too much of the debris of others as though this body doesn't have full awareness of your mission. It would be well to practice much clearing of this debris including the ownership of your own thought forms that dwell in fear and shame. You need not be aligned with physical pain even though you experience it. Be aligned with that which creates "no pain" and therefore doesn't fear pain. You will not need to retreat from your purpose this life; you are already living it. Nothing will be asked of you that you did not agree upon. Again, the pain is an experience of the expectations of itself...this is bad so it must be painful. It can be "bad" and not be painful; it can be "good" and be painful. It is the way of choosing the placement of power. You don't need to rest from the choosing. What you feel you need to rest from are the choices you gave away. It doesn't have to be so.

§§

You are turning in the wrong direction. Bear with us. What you are working with is okay and you need to learn it as it will help you but you try too hard on the intellectual level. Instead, you need to change your focus to that of a spiritual level. Learn to accept the information you are receiving and understand that it will help you if you just accept it. There is a whole other level within yourself that you have not yet tapped You need to access this if you wish to follow your purposeful path. We will help you get through this week and then slow down. You need more quiet time so we can come to you and explain things to you. Be at peace; you are doing the best you can but things get too overwhelming. You need more time in nature to de-stress.

§§

You don't listen. You go off on your own trip. Be still more; be quiet; seek the voice from within. You know it is there but you are not taking sufficient time to hear it. You need to start getting rid of things. You don't need all this stuff. Find ways to reuse or dispose of some of these things. There simply is too much clutter.

§§

All around you are blessings and you will be receiving many more. Hold onto your faith; it serves you well. Yes, your dad was around you yesterday. He was trying to tell you not to get discouraged, that this will all turn out okay. You are blessed and will continue to be blessed. You have much to do and it will all be known to you soon. We are with you always and willing to help you. Your time to be the Wise Woman is near. Keep up your studies so that you may understand all you need to know.

§§

Put your pen to paper, my child and hear Me out. You are a beautiful child of God. You are just fine with all your human frailties. Part of your lessons and struggles are so you understand your human imperfections and learn to be stronger. You are what you are, and God still loves you. Learn to love yourself as much as you are willing to love others in all their imperfectness. Simply learn to take better care of yourself. You deserve it and are worthy of it. Use some of your time more wisely to create a little more time for yourself and spend it in more enjoyable pursuits. You will be glad you did.

§§

This day a door will open for you. Watch closely for it, lest you miss it. I will send what you need but you must be alert. I will put it in your hand, a miracle, but you may not recognize it. Therefore, walk through this day with much awareness. Go, do, but watch! Watch! Watch! Yes, all is well. You do not need to understand all the mysteries; only revealed will be that which you need to know. Be assured I will not fail you; you are My child and abide in My love. Others have made you feel unworthy, but you are Mine. Go forth, with great joy, be glad and know that you are, indeed, loved. I come through you to touch the ordinary, everyday person struggling through life, unable *to find their true way, their path. Just as you have struggled, so do so many others. I come through you to light their way, to tell them they are really okay; they are loved just as you are loved. Don't struggle so hard, just know that I am and I am here to help if you just ask. I am deep within you and so are all the answers.*

Life goes on and is so full of twists and turns that you must choose your path more carefully. Take time to help others, be loving and kind to all My creatures; love yourself. Understand that I am here for you. Rejoice as you wake to each new day. I have made it and it is yours; put it to good use...yours and Mine. I am with you, each step of the way.

There is not one of you, more or less worthy than the other, so yes, I would talk to you. Why not; who else? At the very least you love to create the flow of words from pen across the paper. It is easy to come through you. You have a right heart; you will do well. Rejoice in this day, your birthday. You will count all those that remain as blessings, opportunities to help others and make an impact on the world about you. I tell you this day your purpose is clear, follow it without haste. You still have time. The years have been good to you; you have no bitterness for the past. Things will improve; do not be afraid. There is much to come and it will unfold as it should. Trust Me.

§§

Your intentions are fine but you struggle too much to make them a reality. Learn to relax more and let them just flow into your life as the Divine sees fit. You are still learning and will always be learning more and more. At some point you must make the decision to share what you know. One of your intentions is to help others understand what you already know. Get ready to do it soon. You cannot wait until you think you know all there is to know; your learning will never be finished. Therefore, go with what you already know. The experiences you have will increase your knowledge. You will help others more than you can realize at this time. Keep working with your intentions. You will be successful.

This is the last one I received:

*There is good in all of mankind; a simple theme that bears repeating. The stresses of life reduce your vision. You get so caught up in the mundaneness of all around you, you forget to look for the beauty of the soul. Too much stuff can never fill the emptiness; you look in all the wrong places. God can stand to have you do with less. It is written so in the stars; you are fools in the way you live. Be simple, be clean, love one another, be kind. Look to God for direction. He will give it willingly. There is nothing He cannot do; you have to ask. He has great plans for you but too often they fall on deaf ears. Trust, above all, **trust**. Let go and let God take care of it all. He is not a scheming partner in life, looking to steal everything from you. Oh, no, you will have riches beyond riches, if you but listen to Him. Life takes you where you don't always want to go. Be sure you follow the road that He holds open for you; you will be glad you did. You can find it anytime, anywhere. He is always waiting for you, from birth to the end. If you really listen, you will hear. You have your own ears and your own way of finding Him. Do not follow someone else. They only have their own answers, not yours. You were made whole and perfect; God never sees you as anything less; He welcomes you always and ever. Be aware of those who would beat you down and make you small. God alone is sure of your greatness. Find life's greatest pleasures in the simple things. There is so much joy in the things* *of nature that God has already created. These show you how wonderfully simple life can be. More and bigger just get more complicated and loads all of you down with its burden, taking all your time and energy and leaving you with no real resources, barren within. You can't find God in things, amid the clutter. You can only find Him within, by looking at your uncluttered, simple, loving soul. There He resides ever and always. Go for the gold, the essence of self where all heaven resides.*

CHAPTER XIII

PRAYERS

*Prayer is not a duty or a habit, but a pouring forth of
the heart in gratitude for every breath,
every moment of life, every experience.*
Sue Sikking
A Letter To Adam

The following are prayers that I have written and some of them I
use daily. Please feel free to use any that appeal to you or, better
yet, write your own by just saying what is in your heart.

A PRAYER

Thank You God and Universe for bringing me each day to this
silent time alone with Thee. Help me to fill my days with the best
use of my talents. May I be kind to and patient with all those I
meet. May I rejoice in the bounteous gifts of nature that You have
supplied. May I return again tomorrow.

MY DAILY PRAYER

Heavenly Mother, Father God, Loving Universe, thank You for
bringing me to this new day and all the potential it holds for doing

Thy will. Please show me what it is You would have me do today. Please show me how to best serve You by helping others.

Please help me to forgive everyone for everything including myself; to see everyone as a holy, loving child of God and to be patient, loving and kind to all I come in contact with. I thank you for all the blessings in my life (list at least five).

Please watch over the sick and restore them to health if at all possible, including but not limited to (list them by name). Please bring the dying home swiftly to Your arms and comfort all who grieve their loss, especially those affected by homicides, suicides, natural disasters and bloody conflicts around the world.

Please watch over all those I love and their families, keeping them safe and free from harm, including but not limited to (again, list by name or family).

As always Thy will be done. Thank You, thank You, thank You and so it is.

ANOTHER PRAYER

Reveal to me, oh Great Universe, the path that I need to take; open for me the door that will lead to my true way; let me breathe deeply of the path that is truly mine. Help me to see all that I need to see, understand all that I need to know. Help me unravel all the twists and knots that lay before me. Shine brightly before me on that path that I may find the way even in the darkness that fills my soul. I do not want to fail to find the truth that lies buried deep within me. Please show me how to uncover these mighty treasures; else my life will be for naught.

A SIMPLE PRAYER

Allow me to be empty that I may fill with all that is intended for me this day. Allow me to open and bend with the will far greater than mine. I want to explore what exists on a higher level than this nitty-gritty world. But I also want to rejoice in the ordinariness of life and pass this joy on to others.

Help me to be gracious to all that I come in contact with this day. "How can I help you" should always show through my actions and my words. I need to sweep aside my agenda to make room for the greater purpose to flow through my days. Bless this lowly existence that is me.

REQUESTING ANGELIC HELP

I call now on St. Michael the Archangel, Archangel Gabriel, Archangel Haniel and my spirit guides (name them if you know them) and all the Ascended Masters, Archangels, Angels, Guardians, Guides, Spirits and Fairies to come and surround me for a brief moment while I thank you for all your guidance and protection. I know you are always nearby keeping me safe and free from harm and I love you all. Please be with me this day and through the coming night until I see tomorrow's morning light, guarding and guiding my footsteps and my words. Thank you; thank you; thank you; and so it is.

SHORT PRAYER

I trust that the Universe will provide all that is needed to carry me through this day. I thank the Loving Universe for all that it provides

PRAYER FOR GUIDANCE

Point me toward the heavens, guides and angels; open my heart that I may feel; open my inner ears that I may hear all of you. Let me go deep within to that place where my mysteries are stored. Help me to uncover the knowledge that I need to progress on my true path. Help me to quiet the distractions from my noisy ego and the world at large. Help me to bring peace to my soul and to all those lives I touch. Let me ease their burdens in some manner rather than add to their troubles. Help me to spread love and kindness to all who enter my energy field. I know I am very blessed and provided for. Days are filled with the comings and goings of the positive and negative. Help me to nurture the positive and send the negative back to from whence it came. Above all, keep me humble, for I realize that greater Beings than I are at work here.

CHAPTER XIV

DAILY THOUGHTS

Don't judge each day
by the harvest you reap,
but by the seeds that you plant.
Robert Louis Stevenson
Tiny Buddha

Two months after my youngest son passed away I was motivated to send out a daily message to many people I knew, and as they forwarded this nugget each day to their family and friends, the list has grown. My only purpose in this effort was to try my best to help people think about what is really important in life and to make the most of whatever time they have with those they love. Frankly the idea came from an article I read about a mentally challenged young man, working as a bagger in a grocery store. As he took care of customers' groceries he began adding to their bags a small piece of paper with a daily thought of encouragement. His effort became so popular that customers insisted on standing in his line no matter how long the wait.

I gather quotes from everywhere and am inspired to write many on my own. My suggestion to each of you is to find one message each day that resonates with you for that day; write it down and put it where you can reread it or carry it with you. I've been told that trying to read all of the messages at once to find your truth in the entire chapter can be too confusing. I send them out, one a day, for a reason...to inspire on a daily basis. These are the ones I have written:

**

Fairness has little to do with the reality of life and loving. How you perceive this issue will determine whether you live steeped broadly in love or narrowly in meanness and sorrow.

**

Where are your moments of peace...in the early morning or late evening quiet and solitude...in the midst of some creative project or helping others? Peace inside and out tells you that you are right where God wants you. Work to remain in the flow of the Universe's love.

**

Think and speak calmly with
Only the most positive word.
You will be delighted with
How much better you're heard.

**

There are no greater essentials for living life to the fullest than desire and imagination. Desire is needed to unlock the door of possibility and imagination is required to open the door and look within. All manner of delightful and interesting potentials can be found there. Give yourself permission to fly; remember, even Orville Wright didn't have a pilot's license.

**

I'm in love with peace, with the quiet early morning moments that I seek. Herein lies all the gifts God brings to me, to be shared and echoed throughout my day.

**

Rather than treating life as a to-do list, rejoice in the smallest of blessings. Approach each day and all of life as being filled with possibilities and live each moment to its fullest, simply because some day you won't.

**

Wherever you are in the moment, whether it is optimal or not...remember you and everyone, everything, are in a continually evolving state. Nothing lasts forever. Two days, six weeks, three years, will all find you somewhere else, no doubt with a different view on what you are concerned about today. Life changes all the time and opportunity presents itself in many different ways. So, smile and stay alert...because the "lerts" get the most out of life.

**

Let us begin this day, and every day henceforth, by being grateful for all that is present in our lives right now, especially the little things. They are the constants that keep us flowing in the now. Big things are like fireworks...they only appear now and then. But they would never materialize without the daily presence of those little things.

**

Beneath the hustle and bustle, the gifts and the toys and the happiness of loved ones gathering, can you remember that the real reason that sparks all this craziness is *love*? If not, take 10 to relax and reflect.

**

Yes, even on Christmas Day, someone, somewhere needs a prayer. Please oblige and have a blessed day, everyone.

**

As the year draws to a close I realize it has taught me all over again:

Life is like the river's current, constantly moving, filled with riptides and sunlit ripples alike;

The challenges are never ending, twisting and turning lives upside down sometimes;

As is so often said, it matters not what life hands us but rather, what we do with it that counts and sometimes we can only slosh through it all, up to our armpits, navigating with little direction.

But if we just keep going, eventually we will find that the sun is still shining and life turns a little brighter and easier again.

**

Learning to focus on the simple blessings each day can become a tool that carries us through the darkness. A bird's song, hot soup, coffee, tea, flowers (wherever they bloom), good friends (how could we manage without them), a quiet moment, a hot shower, a good night's sleep, laughter, especially laughter (such a saving grace), a good book or soothing music. We overlook the simple, the humble, but that is what life is made up of. How often do you have a dynamite day or even a fireworks moment?

**

In reality, none of it goes with us except what we carry in our hearts. What are you holding in yours today: love, peace, laughter or is there anger and hate? Put the light of love to work like a lit wick melts a candle. Dispel the darkness and replace it with the light of love and laughter. It won't happen all at once, but pay attention every day long enough to start the flow of love moving through your heart. One day you will realize that the sadness that surrounded all the darkness has melted away and light and love fill your life. Love is all that matters, anyway.

**

Where is this day taking you? It will depend on your thoughts and where you allow them to set your focus: think sad, be sad; think lonely, be lonely; think love, act with love; think peace, dwell in its place; think thankful, wrap yourself in the blanket of life's gifts. Dwell only on what you truly desire to be and to have and all else falls away.

**

My wish for everyone today is a quiet mind, unfettered, free of the zillion ties, burdens, demands that turn us into whirling dervishes. Simply breathe, stretch, breathe, and let all the concerns float up to the hands of God. Free yourself to the quiet that comes when you open and allow.

**

What is the truest desire of your heart in this moment? You are the song seeking the root of truth. Become silent and listen; *trust*.

**

Do you sit in peace each morning even for a few minutes acknowledging the anticipation of all the good and love you can give and receive? Take time to wrap yourself in love so that this gift will grow and glow and extend to all you touch with words and deeds this day.

**

There is no way you can ever move forward if you spend all your time and energy searching for answers in the rear view mirror.

**

How big an act does it take to make a difference in the world? How long does it take? Who knows? Just start small and see what results.

**

Just being kind, patient and helpful to those we interact with on a daily basis can make a difference, large or small, to everyone. For it is the little acts of kindness that add up and bless us all, giver and receiver.

**

Give yourself the daily gift of a few minutes of centered quiet. It will multiply in waves all day long.

**

Creativity...the juice that dreams up the world; the flow that vibrates to become the perfect harmony of your heart's song. Are you juiced?

**

Be the light that erases the darkness. Be the seed of joy that can grow and blossom anywhere and everywhere. Be the mirror that others can reflect in and expand that reflection into their circle of love.

**

Choosing where to focus your energy is key to controlling stress. Ask yourself just how much energy is a particular situation worth?

**

We are all here to write the stories of our lives. If we're less than pleased with the direction the upcoming pages seems to be taking, we still have some time to rewrite. Are you brave enough to start now?

**

Today give yourself a gift...renew your love affair with life.

**

Spread a little light, a little love, a little sunshine, every day in any small way you can.

**

Love is the reason we are here. And when we leave, all we take with us is the love we have given away.

**

The important thing is to acknowledge that there is an all-powerful, loving, healing, presence that accepts you just as you are and is always available to help and guide you, regardless of where you are at any given moment.

**

For where are we if we are not in this moment? The past cannot be rewritten with our tears; the future lays hollow, waiting to be filled by what we do and say now.

**

For it is with our daily thoughts that we shape our very lives.

**

If you meet someone on the path today who is a little (or a lot) less kind or impatient, remember we are not all standing in the same place in terms of spiritual knowledge and experience. Be kind, be patient, act with love, for all will eventually move into the One Place of Understanding.

**

Are you walking the path of least resistance or the more difficult one of most loving persistence?

**

May your Thanksgiving be filled with hugs from those you love and gratefulness for all the blessings, large and small, that we all enjoy every day. Happy Thanksgiving.

**

May peace and love fill your hearts this holiday season. Take time to pause and count all your blessings and hug all who are dear to you.

**

More than ever in this world today we need the love and peace that is the foundation and real meaning of this Christmas season. Let these gifts be renewed and made stronger by each of us.

**

Merry, blessed Christmas and love to all. Rejoice in the presence of loved ones as you gather to celebrate. Remember to pause long enough to send a prayer out to someone in need.

**

Remember that "good works" can be packaged in small ways as well as large. Little kindnesses done often can contain more caring than the occasional big gestures.

**

The flow of who you really are is always there but you may have dammed it up...stick your finger in the dike to poke a hole and let your truth out.

**

This go 'round is all that we know for now. Perhaps we'll come back many more times and may have done so already, but what we have is what we've got here and now...put it to good use.

**

As you open the door to a new year, open it to all you can be. You never know where you'll find yourself 12 months or 10 years from now so make each day matter.

**

May 2013 bless all of you with abundant health, all the love you can share, peace to sustain you and the music that makes your heart sing so that you may share your gifts.

**

Leave the past behind lest it hover around and haunt you. Let it rest, for it is gone. Be here, be now and be present in the moment so that the future will fill itself from today's bounty.

**

There is nothing you can't accomplish when your imagination is fueled by your determination.

**

You're never too old to try something new... you just have to be daring and nuts like me!

**

Make a vow in the unfolding year to uncover a long cherished dream or even find a new one. If the outcome is less than you looked for, at least you tried. And who knows what other roads might open?

**

May we never grow too old to dream, to try something new. In the meantime we can always take a nap.

**

Find the music that awakens your soul so that you can sing a new song that breaths joy into your days.

**

Allow the quiet daily practice of meditation and prayer to bring you to that place of deep knowing within. No matter what the question, the answer is always there.

**

As the long path of grieving continues one unfolds into a place of acceptance, as opposed to the impossible, but longed for restoration of what once was.

**

Do you believe that you are simply the one greatest asset you will ever possess and be in charge of? What are you doing to protect and improve this treasure?

**

Being loved is an answer to prayer. Being loving is a prayer.

**

Can you find the diamonds scattered among the gravel on the road that is your life? Dig deeper, for they are there waiting for you to claim.

**

Life holds living so grab it with all the gusto you can and hold on as long as you can. If you live fully you will know when it is time to let go.

**

If you could say or do just one thing before you go, what would it be? What are you waiting for?

**

In the midst of all tragedy and negative circumstances, goodness and kindness appear spontaneously from all corners to aid those suffering in our midst. Strangers helping strangers...that is America...that is love in action.

**

Each day you are creating a masterpiece. Is it the very best that you are capable of?

**

Today is unique and the only day you have...relish it. Far too quickly life will move you on to other people and places. Nothing is unbearable if managed one day at a time. After 27,200 I have never found two that were exactly alike, either.

**

The tests of life are what uncover your mettle. When you come through them you will better understand what you are made of.

**

When you live your life by your inner guidance you will have no concern for what others think you should do. You know you are creating the path that is directed by your most authentic self.

**

Just think...if Eve hadn't been made from Adam's rib and our mothers hadn't met our fathers...we would all be somebody else!

**

We make each other stronger by leaning on one another.

**

How far can you soar in life? You'll never know until you take that first step out of your comfort zone into the world of endless possibilities. Oh, and age doesn't matter.

If you would like to receive these daily messages please send your request by putting "Daily Messages" in the subject box and emailing to: <u>AgelessSage8@AOL.com.</u>

CHAPTER XV

THE JOURNEY CONTINUES

Now I become myself; It's taken
Time, many years and places;
I have been dissolved and shaken,
Worn other people's faces,
Run madly, as if Time were there,
Terribly old, crying a warning,
"Hurry, you will be dead before—"
(What? Before you reach the morning?
Or the end of the poem is clear?
Or love in the walled city?)
Now to stand still, to be here,
Feel my own weight and density!
——I, the pursued, who madly ran,
Stand still, stand still, and stop the sun!
(excerpt from Now I Become Myself)
May Sarton
Journal of a Solitude

What have I learned from living through all of these losses, all the
grieving, and the restructuring of life as I knew it? I discovered
that in spite of the deepest emotional and mental pain that nearly
defies discription, I still get up each morning. I found my spiritual resources are absolutely rock solid and carry me into a future

that is not only bearable but still holds much laughter and peace. I was awakened more than ever to the value of friends and family who stepped forward in love and caring to offer all their various talents to help sustain me when life crumbled around me. I was amazed at how much resilience and fortitude this little body held. My background, my spiritual base, my genes, my life experiences all melded together to help me work through these challenges. I expect it will always be so.

Grieving is normal and necessary. In a sense we mourn all of life's changes even when they evolve into better circumstances. We all grieve at our own pace. Yet, there does come a time when we need to let it all go in peace and move on. While we are still present and breathing on this earth we have some purpose we are to be fulfilling. We need to get to it rather than allow ourselves to be dead among the living. If necessary, ask for help. There is no shame in having someone, be it a pastor, counselor, etc. help you move through the hard parts into a future that will be different but can still hold joy.

Have I moved on emotionally in the past two years? Yes, by choice. I refused to stay immersed in that deepening abyss that grieving offers. I have pushed myself to rejoin living in peace and joy. Is the grieving over? Not yet, and it may never be. Losses that are this deep don't readily dissolve. Remnants linger in the background and sneak into my awareness without warning, bringing a few unbidden tears as well. But the grief, the overwhelming sense of loss, no longer dominates my days and nights. I have made a very conscious choice to maintain an active, engaged life.

Our grieving does define us, but we can select, with conscious effort, what that definition will be. Don't ever feel you are without options, regardless of where you see yourself at any moment.

Sometimes you just have to be brave enough to make the effort to move on into a more desired place.

I have no fear of dying for I believe that too many wonderful things and my loved ones wait for me on the other side of that thin line. Right now it doesn't feel to me as though that crossing time is very near. I believe, that at long last, having found the best way to make use of my talents, I'll be here a while longer. I'm thinking another twenty or so years should do it.

It has been said that as long as we breathe we are working out our life's purpose. When our job is finished, so are we. I can accept that. No matter what we own or accomplish here I don't believe it can compare to the wonder and spiritual development in store for us when we die. There is still so much learning that awaits us. I expect it to be an interesting transition.

My losses have been difficult and painful to work through. Losing both of my sons was the most heart wrenching. When Michael died, the grief was nearly impossible to bear. David's passing brought me to my emotional knees. To this day I remain amazed as to how I managed to move past it enough to be able to stand again.

Recently I saw this bit of wisdom written by a mother named Jessica: "Having a child is like having a piece of your soul walking around outside your body." This explains to me, better than any other words I have ever read, the deep bond that exists between aware mothers and their children. I can now better understand why, when that piece of your soul goes home without you, ahead of you, that the loss is so very difficult to accept. It also gives deeper explanation as to why no parent wants to outlive their children, ever. Yet it happens every day, somewhere and my heartfelt prayers go out to everyone who walks that devastating path. Time will move us all into a place of acceptance and peace, but only if we allow it. God's love does work magic and is always available to us all.

My journey to peace continues for there can be no expectation of total, final arrival. It is not an easy slide but rather, a moving forward that holds all its importance in making the trek, without promise of any sense of ultimate destination. By holding value in each step, each day, the peace surrounds and upholds all else that I do.

Too many roads across the years found me pushing through to completion, ignoring the majesty of the changing scenery. At the end of some of these roads, exhausted, I discovered far less joy and exultation than I had hoped for. Perhaps it was my intense focus on the goal that propelled me forward, nose to the self-imposed grindstone. Or it may have been my impatient nature and just knowing that I might lose interest before the finish line that pushed me along blinded to everything else. Regardless of the cause and the consequent outcomes I have arrived where I stand today.

In the beginning of my search I did not realize that my seeking would uncover and change so much within myself. I did believe, given enough time, patience and practice I would arrive at the longed for nirvana. Not so! Didn't happen! I have come to understand it will not happen, ever, as long as I still breathe. The fullness of it may only be realized when my eyes are closed for the last time and my soul goes home. Who knows what stretches out past that thin line to the other side? Will all this even matter when I arrive there?

In truth all of it only holds value for me here daily, depending on what I do with the peace I wrap myself in each morning as I rise.

Only by filling myself, my inner being, with its soft supply, can I ward off the outer world's rumblings, dramas, sadness and meanness. I work at it, some days with more success than others. Just knowing that peace can be woven into my days provides me with additional strength and patience. The true importance lies in forgiving myself regularly for my shortcomings and moving into this light with as much serenity as I am capable of.

Creating a well lived life is rather like baking a cake. You really don't know how it will turn out until it is finished. Of course you can always remake the cake if you aren't satisfied with the end result.

With life, we can't tally it up while we are here. We will never understand the full results of all our living until the opportunity no longer exists to make any changes. That is why it is important to make the best of every day that we are privileged to see dawn. Be kind, be loving, be patient with yourself and everyone around you. Always strive to do the best with what you have and keep trying to find the joy and beauty in each day. Life will hand all of us, sooner or later, some sour grapes when we would rather have sweet ones. Given enough time even sour grapes will grow sweeter, so take what is handed and work through it until you come out the other side, wiser and richer for the experience. Living a life with integrity can be difficult in today's world but it is not impossible.

At this point I find a long line of memories trailing my path, some of them not always so welcome. When they pop up in quiet moments or in those dark unyielding hours of the night I respond quickly, with my mantra of "Be here now." This effectively pushes them aside in favor of more positive thoughts. How much better a solution than letting the past turn me into an embittered, discontent, crabby old woman, spewing ugliness out onto every-one and everything.

Life has much to offer but choices have to be made. Just remem-ber, you can never know everything so don't delay decisions until you have all the facts. Besides, nothing is set in granite except your name on your tombstone. If you feel you have made a less than optimal choice, you can still change your mind. It is up to each of us to choose the positive over the negative. Beauty can be life-time deep if we just look for it.

As I have weathered my personal storms, I have come into a fresh place in understanding and love. By relating these experiences and losses I have hoped to help you, my readers, understand that not only are you not alone, but you can survive, no matter what dark place you may find yourself in.

It is a struggle that, for me, continues. As the years pass, the pain is not as raw. These are the life events that I am learning to accom-modate even if I can never fully recover from them. Life will not go back to where it was. That would be impossible. But life is for the living and so I have chosen to move on. I wrap all that has hap-pened around me and absorb what meaning it holds for me now.

Please realize that you also can continue, perhaps with more pur-pose than ever before. So much good does rise from tragedy every day. It restores our faith in God and man. Learn to be at peace with it all. It seems to be the only way to keep going and build to the future. Don't give up the search for the joy in life that is still here. It does exist.

Before I close I want to add this: a study at Harvard confirms what I've maintained for some time. The study examined the five most important components that Harvard graduates found lead to a truly happy life by following them for 75 years. Number one turned out to be: *Love is really all that matters.*

Please let me know how my story has helped you. You can email me at: <u>AgelessSage8@AOL.com</u>. I would love to hear from you.

Made in the USA
Charleston, SC
20 October 2013